THE BEATLES VS THE ROLLING STONES

SIDE 1

33⅓ RPM

SOUND OPINIONS ON THE
GREAT ROCK 'N' ROLL RIVALRY

WHAT WOULD YOU RATHER BE . . .

A BEATLE . . .

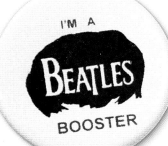

I'M A

Beatles

BOOSTER

MEMBER

beaTles

FAN CLUB

I'M A
BEATLE FAN
In Case of EMERGENCY
CALL **PAUL**
OR **RINGO**

I Love the Stones

THE WORLD'S GREATEST ROCK 'N ROLL BAND

I ♥ MICK JAGGER

I slept with Keith Richards

THE ROLLING STONES

. . . OR A STONE?

JIM DeROGATIS & GREG KOT

THE
BEATLES

VS

THE
ROLLING
STONES

SOUND OPINIONS ON THE GREAT
ROCK 'N' ROLL RIVALRY

Voyageur
Press

First published in 2010 by Voyageur Press, an imprint of MBI Publishing Company, 400 First Avenue North, Suite 300, Minneapolis, MN 55401 USA

Voyageur Press titles are also available at discounts in bulk quantity for industrial or sales-promotional use. For details write to Special Sales Manager at MBI Publishing Company, 400 First Avenue North, Suite 300, Minneapolis, MN 55401 USA.

To find out more about our books, visit us online at www.voyageurpress.com.

ISBN-13: 978-0-7603-3813-1

Library of Congress Cataloging-in-Publication Data

DeRogatis, Jim.
  The Beatles vs. the Rolling Stones : sound opinions on the great rock 'n' roll rivalry / Jim DeRogatis and Greg Kot.
      p. cm.
  Includes bibliographical references and index.
  ISBN 978-0-7603-3813-1 (plc)
 1. Beatles–Criticism and interpretation. 2. Rolling Stones–Criticism and interpretation. 3. Rock music–1961-1970–History and criticism. I. Kot, Greg. II. Title.
  ML3534.D466 2010
  782.42166092'241–dc22
                              2010003192

Editor: Dennis Pernu
Design Manager: Katie Sonmor
Cover Design and Layout: John Barnett/4 Eyes Design
Timeline Design: Erin Fahringer and John Barnett/4 Eyes Design

Printed in China

CONTENTS

WHO'S COOLER, THE BEATLES OR THE ROLLING STONES?

This is a question that's been posed as the start of an always hard-fought but generally good-natured game played by super-geek rock fans around the world for half a century, and it took my colleague Greg Kot and me about one second to answer the first time we were asked by Voyageur Press editor Dennis Pernu.

The Stones, of course! *Duh.*

Needless to say, we both think the Fab Four was a pretty great band, too, but it's all in the way you ask the question. If we're talking who was *cooler* during that legendary rivalry in the Sixties, there's really no contest, as the Stones pretty much defined the term—see Mick Jagger's strut, Keith Richards' slouch, Brian Jones' sleepy-eyed sneer, the unshakeable stoicism of Charlie Watts and Bill Wyman, et cetera, et cetera, *ad infinitum.* If, however, you ask which band has had more far-ranging or enduring influence; which was stronger or more innovative in the recording studio versus being more electrifying onstage; which caused the bigger social impact; which boasted the more ambitious songwriters, more effective singers, more virtuosic musicians, or any of a thousand other variations . . . well, now you've got a championship match, and that's what Dennis really had in mind.

Greg and I already had contributed album-appreciation essays to Voyageur's beautiful coffee-table books on Led Zeppelin and Queen, and I had edited and written the central historical essay for their tome on the Velvet Underground, which also included a contribution from Mr. Kot. When Dennis posed the "Beatles or Stones?" query to us during a visit to Minneapolis and asked if we'd be interested in a book-length response, it made sense that he came to us: In addition to serving as the ever-competitive rock critics at the *Chicago Tribune* (Greg) and, until early 2010, the *Chicago Sun-Times* (Jim), we are the consistently contentious co-hosts of *Sound Opinions*, a public radio program that we proudly call "the world's only rock 'n' roll talk show"—in the tradition of the Stones as "the world's only rock 'n' roll band" or the Lester Bangs–era *Creem* as "the world's only rock 'n' roll magazine." We disagree with one another about myriad musical issues constantly, week in and week out, and even when we're on the same page about an artist's assets or demerits, it's invariably for different reasons.

Truth be told, we didn't instantly embrace Dennis' idea. Dedicated students of rock history and avid readers of the canon of rock literature, we were dubious that the world needed another book about either of these bands when so many great ones already have been written. Certainly neither of us wanted to force taking a hard-and-fast "anti-" position on either of two bands we both deeply love; in the end, the only real answer to the question "Beatles or Stones?" is "Both!" But if Dennis betrayed a momentary flash of disappointment that the two of us didn't instantly divide into one pro-Beatles / anti-Stones guy and vice versa, that disappeared as we spent the next hour arguing the finer points of exactly how and why one band had it all over the other on this, that, or the other thing. (Jim: "*Their Satanic Majesties Request* is, hands down, a better psychedelic rock album than *Sgt. Pepper's Lonely Hearts Club Band*!" Greg: "You're nuts! You're gonna tell me that 'In Another Land' is half as good a song as 'A Day in the Life'? How do you come up with this crap?") That argument continued through the rest of our visit, in the airport as we were leaving, during the plane ride home, and during breaks in our next radio taping—and it's still going strong today, even now that we've filled up Dennis' book.

Here, I will cease putting words in my partner's mouth to note that what finally convinced me of the worth of this project, however silly it might initially have seemed, was the way our back-and-forth dialog about these two legendary bands prompted me to reconsider long-held convictions. (Kot has a way of doing that to me, but don't tell him I said that.) Suddenly, I was rushing back to well-worn recordings to listen anew with fresh ears, diving into dog-eared books I'd already read three times, and watching movies in which I already knew every line of dialogue by heart (Man on train: "Don't take that tone with me, young man. I fought the war for your sort." Ringo: "I bet you're sorry you won."), searching for fresh fodder to bolster my points, and plain and simple getting all hot and bothered about both the Beatles *and* the Stones with more passion and enthusiasm than I'd had since I'd first discovered them as a preteen.

Let's face it: At this point, Lennon, McCartney, Jagger, and Richards are the Mount Rushmore of Rock. Together with their band mates, they're revered deities whose infallibility is never questioned and whose genius is taken as a given, and hence is taken for granted. They're also the ultimate nostalgic touchstones for a generation—the Baby Boomers', not mine. I'm on the cusp of Generation X, so I discovered the Fabs via the red and blue "best-of" albums and *Beatlemania* at the Wintergarden Theatre on Broadway; *Some Girls* was the first Stones album I bought when it was released. The Beatles and the Stones are also money-minting corporate entities endlessly repackaging and reselling their wares via any medium you care to name, from the soundtracks of obnoxious television commercials to glitzy Las Vegas stage shows, and from covers by the likes of weird pop novelties such as Susan Boyle to much-hyped special-edition video games. And, sadly, all of this unquestioning hero worship, commercial white noise, and pop-culture ubiquity can make it hard to actually hear what's so incredible about the music, though incredible it is and will remain.

In the end, if our arguments, rendered in prime *Sound Opinions* style, make you curse one or the other of us as you consider hurling this book across the room, then so be it—so long as you're also prompted to go back to these bands' recordings, because that's really what it's all about. And when you get there, we hope you have half as much fun as the two of us always do.

PREFACE

BY GREG KOT

THERE ARE CERTAIN THINGS WE GROW UP HEARING

over and over again from our elders: the older brothers and sisters in their you-shoulda-been-there all-knowingness, the uncle who went to Woodstock and danced naked in the mud with someone named Chelsea Flowerchild, the Boomers in the media who have monopolized the discussion about culture and music since the Sixties. One of those bromides is the enduring greatness of the Beatles and the Stones. Of course, if you were a Sixties kid, it had to be one or the other, never both: Not Beatles *and* Stones, but Beatles *vs.* Stones.

I was a touch too young to appreciate these bands in their heyday, and by the time I became a full-on music fanatic in the mid-Seventies, punk ruled our teenage corner of the world and Boomer bands were out. The only Sixties bands that mattered were the Velvet Underground, the Stooges, the MC5, and bratty outsiders and one-hit wonders like the Seeds, the Trashmen, and the Standells. The Beatles were no longer recording, and the solo albums of John, Paul, George, and Ringo barely registered. "Phony Beatlemania!" the Clash's Joe Strummer sneered at the way these Sixties icons were consistently repackaged, resold, and restuffed down a new generation's throat.

The Stones should've been equally off-putting. By the mid-Seventies they had become jet-set celebrities, sure, but they remained somehow outside the margins of corporate rock even as they were rolling in the dough. When they put out *Some Girls* in 1978, they reminded everyone why they were the original rock 'n' roll badasses. I was hooked, particularly in thrall to Keith Richards, the original punk rocker, and Charlie Watts, who seemed even cooler than Keith, if that was possible. I had posters of the sullen, leather-clad

Ramones and the androgynous, leering Stones on my bedroom wall, and my mother demanded that I remove the Stones poster because it scared her—which only confirmed that my fandom was not misplaced.

As dormitory friends in college with cool record collections blew my mind on a nightly basis with the music of Bob Dylan, Marvin Gaye, Love, Sam & Dave, and other Sixties artists alongside our beloved Patti Smith, Television, Roxy Music, New York Dolls, and Iggy Pop, Beatlemania finally invaded my head. Hearing "A Hard Day's Night" at a listening party one foggy evening, it hit me all at once: The Beatles rocked! What took me so long? That opening chord—one George Harrison chord—and you knew instantly who it was and that you needed to hear more. The architecture of that arrangement, the ridiculous hooks, the exuberant melody lines, the harmonies—wow!

And now, here we are thirty years later, and I'm coauthoring a book about two bands as ubiquitous as oxygen, their music still with us long after many of their peers have become period pieces. My *Sound Opinions* colleague Jim DeRogatis and I don't agree on much when it comes to music, but we're both intent on tossing out the received wisdom, the cultural baggage that's been passed down from generation to generation, and judging the music on its own merits—what it says to us today. We're not of the belief that it was all said and done in the Sixties and Seventies and that everything since has been just a hollow echo of that Golden Age. On the contrary, we believe the music that is being made today is every bit as moving and powerful. If anything, the onus is on the Golden Age bands to demonstrate why we should still care. How many times have we run back to an album or song we once held dear because

it reminds us of a certain period in our lives, only to find that the music—removed from its personal and cultural context—doesn't quite hold up?

When our editor, Dennis Pernu, approached us about taking on the greatest of rock 'n' roll rivalries, manufactured or not, the notion was initially daunting: Hasn't everything already been said about these bands—twice? But then we became intrigued by the opportunity to examine the bands side by side, to indulge in the ultimate rock 'n' roll fantasy game, to join a debate that has been going on for decades but that never has had a book devoted to it. What's more, it allowed us to dive into the music, rediscover it for ourselves, and determine what it means today. Could a new fan in 2010 get the same thrill out of the music that a teen in 1966 got when hearing *Revolver* or *Aftermath* for the first time? Has the music grown up with the listeners who first experienced it when it was new? Does it epitomize nostalgia or transcend it?

If anything, I came away from this experience more in awe than ever of what the Beatles and the Stones have accomplished. DeRo and I aren't shy about pointing out flaws and failings (some folks might justifiably call it nitpicking), but I hope the primary emotion conveyed is one of joy—the joy of rediscovering something wonderful and finding new facets of it to celebrate. We'd spend a few weeks listening to and researching a particular period in the careers of the Beatles and Stones, and then convene to talk about it. The dialogues you read in this book are transcriptions of our real-time conversations, and I hope as you scan the words, you can also feel the excitement in our voices. To you, the readers, I hope this book will be as enriching to your music-listening as writing it was to ours.

MYTH-MAKING 101

1

MOP TOPS IN MATCHING SUITS vs. "WOULD YOU LET YOUR SISTER GO WITH A ROLLING STONE?"

JD: As we look at the perplexing question of which was the cooler band, the Beatles or the Rolling Stones, I think we need to start at the beginning, both in terms of the history as well as the images that both groups were expert in creating. The essential paradox is that the Stones would excel at positioning themselves as the baddest bad boys of rock 'n' roll—"Would you let your sister go with a Rolling Stone?"—while the Beatles were positioned as endlessly cute, cuddly, and lovable—the acceptable face of the counterculture for blue hairs and little kids alike. Yet, the Beatles had a rough-and-tumble upbringing as lower-middle-class if not lower-class kids on the streets of Liverpool—by no means a cultural mecca—and the key players in the Stones had pretty privileged upbringings.

Mick Jagger was from a middle-class family, and he went to Wentworth Primary School in Dartford, where he met Keith Richards. Keith ended up going to Sidcup Art College, while Jagger enrolled at the London School of Economics. And Brian Jones was better off than both of them: He grew up in the provinces, fairly coddled as a grammar-school boy at Cheltenham, and a model student who aced his exams. That's not the case for the Fab Four!

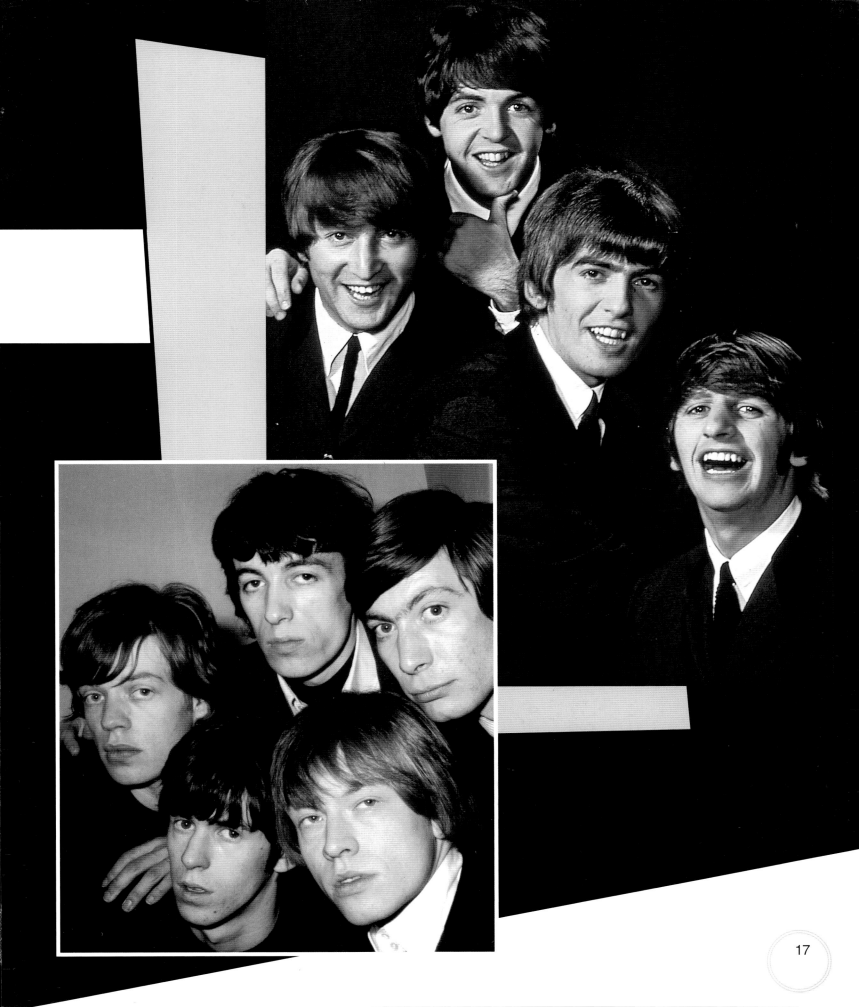

A youngster strolls past a nightclub in Hamburg's notorious Reeperbahn.

Oozing attitude: the Beatles at the Hamburg Funfair. From left: Pete Best, George Harrison, John Lennon, Paul McCartney, and Stuart Sutcliffe.

GK: Early Beatles history sometimes gets written out, but when they were learning how to be a band at those clubs in Hamburg, they were in the den of iniquity, the Babylon of rock 'n' roll, a prostitution center of Germany.

JD: I've been to the Reeperbahn, Hamburg's red-light district, and it's a trip! I grew up across the Hudson River from New York City, and I've got to say that Times Square at its seediest, before it was cleaned up and turned into a Disney-esque shopping mall, had nothing on the Reeperbahn! There, you could walk down the street and see girls half-naked in the windows, cheerfully snorting drugs while waiting for their next john!

GK: You look at the pictures from the Beatles in that era, with the leather jackets, black jeans, T-shirts. . . . They had every bit of the attitude oozing from them in the early, early days that the Stones did when they surfaced. However, it was out of the public limelight. They were playing frenetic sets jacked up on speed. It was crude, lewd, punky—everything the Stones would later be portrayed as embodying. The differences in terms of image would be shaped and dramatized later by their respective managers. Understand the differences between Brian Epstein and Andrew "Loog" Oldham, and you understand how these bands were packaged, marketed, and presented to the world. The truth wasn't necessarily obscured, but it was manipulated for public consumption. Malcolm McLaren, manager of the Sex Pistols, had nothing on these guys. In fact, he probably learned a hell of a lot by studying how Oldham turned the Stones into villains.

A critical difference was that Epstein was born in 1934 and Oldham in 1944, ten years apart. Oldham actually worked public relations in the very early days of the Beatles as they were breaking out of the Liverpool scene, so he saw firsthand the spin that Epstein was putting on the Beatles' image. Oldham came up in the same postwar generation as the Stones. He was a contemporary, whereas Epstein came off as more of an uncle, an elder voice of reason and experience. The swinging London of 1962–1965 was Oldham's world.

Performing at the Cavern Club, Liverpool, February 1961.

He grew up with rock 'n' roll as his soundtrack. Epstein, on the other hand, was a music snob. He managed a record store in Liverpool, and he didn't much like rock 'n' roll. He preferred classical music. But he saw the Beatles play at the Cavern Club, and he loved not so much what he heard but what he saw and felt—the aura and excitement around the band, and the way that young people reacted to them. The Beatles looked and acted like "rough trade," and Epstein saw that this was not just about music but about a certain charisma and sexuality that had appeal for both men and women. All they needed was a little coaching and polishing, and Epstein understood polishing. He got them to wear matching suits, to structure their set lists, to give the unison bow at the end of each show. The Beatles were skeptical at first, but they also saw Epstein as a successful businessman who could take them places they couldn't go without help from a grownup.

Finally, Epstein and Oldham led the bands to a couple of crucial lineup decisions. Epstein brought the Beatles to another pro, producer George Martin, and

Martin, in turn, said the Beatles needed to get rid of Pete Best as the drummer. He couldn't keep up with the other guys. Best was out, and Ringo Starr was in—in retrospect, a key contribution to their sound. Similarly, Oldham pushed really hard to get Charlie Watts in the Stones. It's easy to diss the managers and say they were manipulative, but some of those hard calls early on helped these bands get to where they wanted to be. By 1967, their influence on the bands had diminished considerably. Oldham left the Stones because he hated *Their Satanic Majesties Request*. He said, "I don't even understand you guys anymore."

JD: "You have lost the plot."

GK: I'm not sure the Stones understood themselves anymore at that point, either. Then Epstein died in 1967. It truly was the end of an era for both bands when these two once-all-powerful managers outlived their usefulness. But for those four to five years early on, the Beatles and the Stones wouldn't have been the same without Oldham and Epstein behind the scenes.

Lennon prepares to meet the Queen Mother after asking her to rattle her jewelry at the Royal Variety Performance, Prince of Wales Theatre, London, November 4, 1963.

Disc Weekly reports on the lovable mop tops accepting their MBEs, October 30, 1965.

An elder voice of reason and experience. Beatles manager Brian Epstein with the Beatles at Buckingham Palace after they received their MBEs, October 26, 1965.

JD: It's always hard for us as Americans who were not even contemporaries of these movements to judge how they were viewed at the moment—to put ourselves back in postwar London and understand what Great Britain was like at the time. Plus, as Americans, we don't understand the British class system or how that was affected by the U.K. coming within a hair of falling to the Nazis not all that long before these musicians were born. America, in comparison, was the Wild West. It embraced James Dean and the early rock 'n' rollers, and it wasn't all that threatening, really, to strike a rebellious pose in the United States. But it meant something different in the British Isles in 1961 or 1962, and I'm guessing it was a lot more dangerous. And let's not forget that Jones, in the ultimate bit of button-pushing, eventually donned an SS uniform in a publicity photo.

To what extent was Epstein cleaning up the Beatles because he was afraid that they could not succeed if they did what they wanted to do and let their true badass selves show? They wanted to be the leather-jacketed rock 'n' rollers from America whom they admired. My favorite story of the Reeperbahn excesses in Hamburg was when Lennon was speeding out of his mind and picking fights with the American sailors who populated those bars if they weren't paying proper attention to his band. He was Johnny Rotten long before there was a Johnny Rotten. How does *that* get turned into this erudite, literate, quip-happy character we come to meet on the album covers, in interviews, and in the movies?

GK: Ambition. There was an incredible ambition at the core of it. Lennon could be cynical and rebellious, but he was also the guy exhorting the Beatles to be "the toppermost of the poppermost." So in November 1963, less than a year after he's tearing up Hamburg's seediest nightlife district, he's in a suit and tie performing for the Queen Mother and Princess Margaret at the Royal Variety Performance. How did it get to that point so quickly? All day long before that performance he was rehearsing a line he wanted to use on stage: "The people in the cheap seats clap your hands, the rest of you just rattle your fucking jewelry." Epstein was begging him to reconsider. "Please, John, tone it down! This is our big break." And Lennon *did* tone it down: He said the line, but he deleted the word "fucking." It came off as a quip rather than as an affront or an attack on the queen.

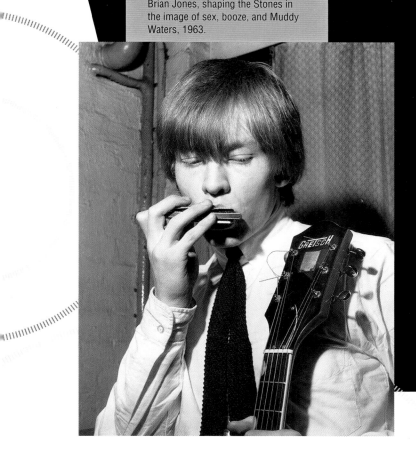

Brian Jones, shaping the Stones in the image of sex, booze, and Muddy Waters, 1963.

Andrew Loog Oldham, representin'.

JD: In front of the Queen, it would have been worse than what the Sex Pistols did with Bill Grundy on the BBC a decade and a half later.

GK: Exactly.

JD: To some extent, you could argue that the Beatles' cultural rebellion was all the more effective for being subdued and couched in the image of the "lovable mop tops." I mean, the Stones were easily dismissed as thugs and ruffians, despite Jagger coming from the London School of Economics. But the Beatles were the guerillas who crept in under the barbed wire and infiltrated the enemy camp. You see that again and again, from "Rattle your jewelry," to smoking pot before they accept their MBEs from the Queen, to "We're more popular than Jesus now"—which is, let's face it, aside from the shock value, one of the more profound cultural criticisms of the Sixties. Lennon knew exactly what he was saying: "How can it be that a pop band now has the cultish devotion and mindless worship that was once accorded solely to religious figures?" That's a sophisticated commentary. It was brilliant in a lot of ways, but still, the Stones' brand of outrage was just . . . *more fun*.

GK: Oh, the Beatles were a lot of fun too, but the Stones were more overt in their love of music that was considered extreme, sexual, and not made for innocent Caucasian adolescents. Just as Lennon defined the Beatles' mission early on, Brian Jones shaped the Stones. When Jagger and Richards met him, Jones was already playing with some of the hardcore blues guys in the London scene, and he had fathered a couple of kids—he was a way cooler guy than anyone they knew. He was like a hip older brother, introducing his siblings to an outlaw world of sex, booze, and Muddy Waters. His mission statement was, "We're going to play authentic Chicago rhythm and blues music." And he named the Rolling Stones after a Waters song. The London blues scene at the time was dominated by older, thirty-something white guys like Cyril Davies, Alexis Korner, and John Mayall. They were aficionados who really knew their Chicago blues, but they weren't all that exciting in terms of how they presented the music. They were very studied and reverential. Into this scene stepped the Stones, who saw the music as a liberating thing—a doorway into a man's world, with all the hedonistic pleasures that implied.

"Bullshit movement," so sayeth Lennon. Jagger does the hip-shake thing.

JD: There was an element to the first-wave British blues scene that was very academic. It was like these college professors and students studying and dissecting an alien music and culture. Whereas the Stones, intuitively or as a well-honed plan, realized that one of the things that was exciting about going to the South Side of Chicago to see Muddy Waters play was that it was just a little bit *dangerous*. It was a sexy, illicit thrill. In their own white, upper-middle-class, English schoolboy way, they began to appropriate that vibe.

GK: Absolutely. Jagger was sitting in with Blues Incorporated, and Cyril Davies would call him "Marilyn Monroe." Here is this guy who is poofing it up and wiggling his hips. When Lennon first saw Jagger perform, there was a bit of envy and jealousy. He called

Jagger's flamboyance "bullshit movement"—mere showmanship. His attitude was that the Beatles left that behind in Hamburg; he was already under the sway of Epstein. Oldham, on the other hand, was talking slang and wearing eye makeup, and he defined the Stones as the anti-Beatles. He knew the Stones couldn't top the Beatles by emulating them, so they would play their opposites. They would use contempt and scandal as marketing devices. The Beatles, as directed by Epstein, were up there shaking their mop tops and smiling for the audience, and the Stones were being characterized as "cavemen" and "apes" in the music press. There was a certain antisocial aspect to the Stones that Oldham embraced and amplified. Jones, for example, couldn't keep a straight day job because he was stealing stuff, and Richards got them kicked out of the Marquee Club

The Stones—all sullen stares and close-ups of Richards' acne.

in London in 1962 because he started a fight with some of the bouncers. Oldham saw this behavior as an image-enhancing asset.

JD: How much of it do you think was a well thought-out plan by Oldham, and how much of it was just him losing his head in the same rough-and-tumble sex, drugs, and rock 'n' roll excesses as the boys he allegedly was "handling"? Epstein was a manager in the real sense; he had a firm grip on the reins, and for a long time, very little happened that he didn't want to happen. He chose those matching suits. He controlled the image on television and in print. He approved which appearances the group made and which invitations it refused. Despite reading Oldham's autobiography, which is entertaining, it's hard to tell how much he was in control. He'll take

credit for things, but I get the sense that he was just one of the guys carousing as much as the others.

GK: No doubt. And if you compare those early Stones records to the Beatles records, it's remarkable how different they are, both in terms of sound and presentation. The Stones' album covers are dark, dank, and not particularly attractive: the sullen stares, the close-ups of Keith's acne. And the sound—with Oldham listed as "producer"—is equally murky. Those records sound almost primitive next to the very polished sound that Epstein was able to give the Beatles by pairing them with Martin and his lab-coated technicians at Abbey Road Studios.

NEMS ENTERPRISES PRESENT AT
NEW BRIGHTON TOWER
FOR ONE NIGHT ONLY 7·30 to 11·30
FRIDAY. JUNE 14th.
"*Merseyside's Greatest...*"
THE BEATLES
AND
GERRY and the PACEMAKERS
TICKETS **6/-** IN ADVANCE
AT DOOR ON NIGHT **7/-**
PLUS 5 GREAT SUPPORTING GROUPS!!
A BOB WOOLER PRODUCTION
DON'T MISS
FRIDAY, JUNE 28th.
JET HARRIS & TONY MEEHAN

6:30 And 8:40
GAUMONT WOLVERHAMPTON
Manager : J. ALEXANDER   Phone : 22534
THURSDAY, 14th MARCH, 1963 ONE DAY ONLY
ON THE STAGE
ARTHUR HOWES presents (in association with EVELYN TAYLOR)
AMERICA'S EXCITING
CHRIS MONTEZ
'LET'S DANCE' 'SOME KINDA FUN'
AMERICA'S FABULOUS
TOMMY ROE
'SHEILA'
The TERRY YOUNG SIX
GLAMOROUS DEBBIE LEE PARLOPHONE
· YOUR 208 D.J. TONY MARSH
The VISCOUNTS PYE RECORDING STARS
BRITAIN'S DYNAMIC
BEATLES
'LOVE ME DO' 'PLEASE PLEASE ME'

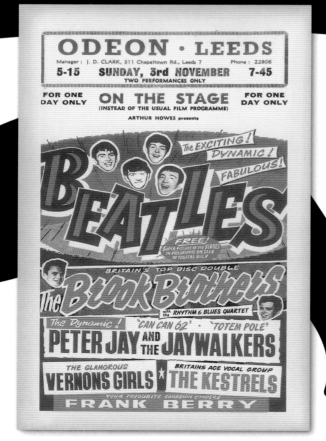

ODEON · LEEDS
Manager : J. D. CLARK, 311 Chapeltown Rd., Leeds 7   Phone : 22806
5-15 SUNDAY, 3rd NOVEMBER 7-45
TWO PERFORMANCES ONLY
FOR ONE DAY ONLY   ON THE STAGE   FOR ONE DAY ONLY
(INSTEAD OF THE USUAL FILM PROGRAMME)
ARTHUR HOWES presents
The EXCITING! DYNAMIC! FABULOUS!
BEATLES
FREE! Super picture of the Beatles in programme on sale at theatre only
BRITAIN'S TOP DISC DOUBLE
The Brook Brothers
with the RHYTHM & BLUES QUARTET
The Dynamic! "CAN CAN 62" "TOTEM POLE"
PETER JAY AND THE JAYWALKERS
THE GLAMOROUS VERNONS GIRLS ★ BRITAINS ACE VOCAL GROUP THE KESTRELS
YOUR FAVOURITE CANADIAN COMPERE
FRANK BERRY

LEACH ENTERTAINMENTS PRESENT
OPERATION BiG BEAT - 5TH
AT THE
TOWER BALLROOM NEW BRIGHTON
FRI. 14TH SEPT. 7·30 - 1·0 A.M.
FEATURING AN ALL STAR 6 GROUP LINE UP · STARRING
THE NORTH'S TOP ROCK COMBO. APPEARING AT 10·30 PROMPT
The BEATLES
RORY STORM with the Hurricanes
GERRY and the PACEMAKERS
THE 4 JAYS
BILLY KRAMER with the COASTERS
THE MERSEY BEATS
TICKETS 5/-
★ LICENSED BARS (UNTIL 12·15 A.M.)
★ LATE TRANSPORT (ALL AREAS L'POOL & WIRRAL)
COACHES LEAVE ST. JOHNS LANE/LIME ST. 7·00-8·30 P.M.
FROM
RUSHWORTHS · NEMS · CRANES · STROTHERS
LEWIS'S · TOP HAT RECORD BAR · TOWER BALLROOM

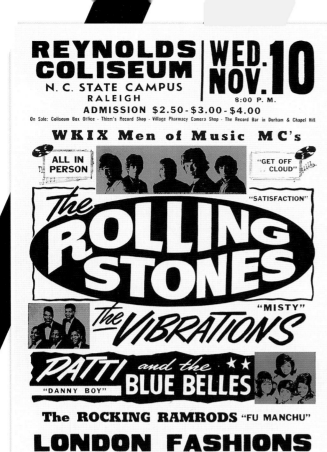

REYNOLDS COLISEUM | WED. NOV. 10
N.C. STATE CAMPUS RALEIGH | 8:00 P.M.
ADMISSION $2.50 - $3.00 - $4.00
On Sale: Coliseum Box Office - Thiem's Record Shop - Village Pharmacy Camera Shop - The Record Bar in Durham & Chapel Hill
WKIX Men of Music MC's
ALL IN PERSON | "GET OFF CLOUD"
"SATISFACTION"
THE ROLLING STONES
"MISTY"
THE VIBRATIONS
PATTI and the BLUE BELLES
"DANNY BOY"
The ROCKING RAMRODS "FU MANCHU"
LONDON FASHIONS BY ELLISBERG'S

"Gather no Moss" WITH
THE ROLLING STONES
JAMES BROWN and the FLAMES
THE SUPREMES · THE BEACH BOYS
CHUCK BERRY · GERRY and the PACEMAKERS
FROM LOS ANGELES TO LIVERPOOL THE WORLD'S BEAT STARS TOGETHER IN ONE GREAT FILM!

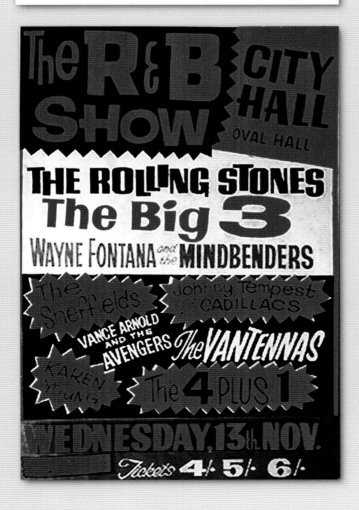

THE R & B SHOW | CITY HALL
OVAL HALL
THE ROLLING STONES
The Big 3
WAYNE FONTANA and the MINDBENDERS
The Sheffields | Johnny Tempest CADILLACS
VANCE ARNOLD AND THE AVENGERS | The VANTENNAS
KAREN YOUNG | The 4 PLUS 1
WEDNESDAY, 13th NOV.
Tickets 4/- 5/- 6/-

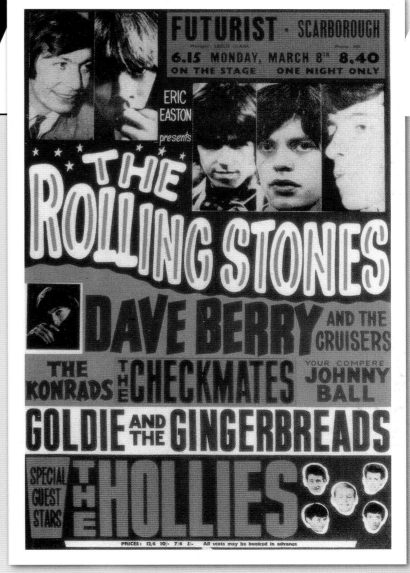

FUTURIST · SCARBOROUGH
6.15 MONDAY, MARCH 8th 8.40
ON THE STAGE | ONE NIGHT ONLY
ERIC EASTON presents
THE ROLLING STONES
DAVE BERRY AND THE CRUISERS
THE KONRADS | THE CHECKMATES | YOUR COMPERE JOHNNY BALL
GOLDIE AND THE GINGERBREADS
SPECIAL GUEST STARS THE HOLLIES
PRICES: 12/6 10/- 7/6 5/- All seats may be booked in advance

Entering the Hippodrome, Birmingham, England, November 10, 1963.

The opening shots in the Beatles' album discography, 1963.

JD: If we're looking at this chronologically, the Beatles' *Please Please Me* comes out in March 1963 in the U.K., and *With the Beatles* follows that November—those are the two opening shots in the band's album discography. If we accept what you're saying, that the Stones were consciously trying to go in the opposite direction from the Beatles, clearly they had time to digest those first two Beatles albums and consider where to zag when the Beatles zigged. The Stones didn't fire their first two shots across the bow until 1964, with their first self-titled release in the U.K. that April—eventually issued in the U.S. in May as *The Rolling Stones (England's Newest Hit Makers)*—and *12x5* coming out in the U.K. that October.

GK: It's telling that the Stones went to Chess Records in Chicago to record the first chance they got when they arrived in America in July 1964. It was another way of distinguishing themselves from what the Beatles were doing.

JD: Well, having spent most of my professional life as a critic in Chicago, I've always wondered about that story of the Stones showing up at Chess. How much of it is myth? Was Muddy Waters really painting the studio when they arrived? And what did the folks at Chess

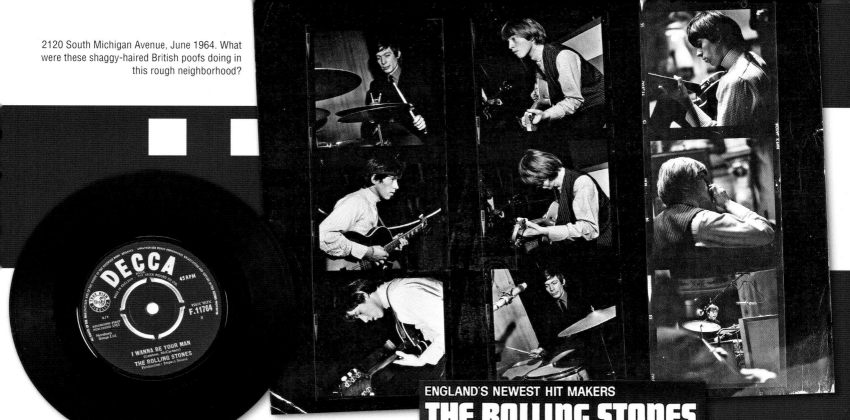

2120 South Michigan Avenue, June 1964. What were these shaggy-haired British poofs doing in this rough neighborhood?

"I Wanna Be Your Man," written by Lennon/McCartney at Andrew Loog Oldham's request.

ENGLAND'S NEWEST HIT MAKERS

Zigging where the Beatles zagged: the Stones' first two LPs, 1964.

really think when these shaggy-haired poofs from the U.K. pulled up and got out of the limo?

GK: They were amused and bemused. Buddy Guy told me he was more curious about what these dudes were doing in this rough neighborhood. He was born in 1936, so he was slightly older than the Stones, but only by a few years. But whatever skepticism the Chicago blues musicians had about the Stones was satisfied when these English guys started playing. The Stones were playing Chicago blues with gusto and sincerity, and it was taken as a compliment: "These white kids from thousands of miles away know our songs?" This is way before the Internet. You had to make a real effort to find out about certain kinds of music, and the Stones had clearly done their homework, so they earned the respect of the blues guys.

But Oldham still had his ties with the Beatles camp, and he respected them and their success. He even solicited a song from the Beatles: "I Wanna Be Your Man" was written by Lennon and McCartney for the Stones at Oldham's request. It's also interesting that the Stones' first U.S. hit wasn't an R&B cover but a song modeled on the Beatles' pop Merseybeat sound: the Jagger-Richards song "Tell Me (You're Coming Back)."

Sacred texts in the Far East, too. This Japanese booklet included two flexi-discs featuring "Ask Me Why," "Please, Please, Me" [*sic*], "She Loves You," and "I Want To Hold Your Hand."

Producer George Martin steering the lads toward more adult fare than the R&B on which they honed their chops.

JD: Pop culture and hero worship have so positioned those early records by both of these bands as sacred texts that at this point, it's hard to really hear them clearly. When I listen to them and remove the burdens of history and mythology, the Beatles often sound hesitant on the first couple of albums, as if they're eager to run but someone is holding them back. It's there in the overly polite approach of the album covers, it's there in Lennon's demeanor—I mean, when you know what he's capable of, to hear him singing Burt Bacharach's "Baby It's You" on *Please Please Me*, you have to wonder, "What is *that* about?" Even if he had never done anything again after that recording, you would listen to it

and say, "I don't think this guy really wants to be singing this song."

GK: There is an awful lot of schmaltz on those early Beatles records. You also have peaks like "I Saw Her Standing There" and that amazing version of "Twist and Shout," where Lennon is fighting a bad cold and tearing his throat up. That performance still makes the hairs on the back of my neck stand up.

JD: Definitely. The opening and closing of *Please Please Me* gives us two of the greatest rock vocal performances ever. But in between on the Beatles' first album, there's

While there was some overlap in the songwriters the two bands chose to cover (notably Chuck Berry, Arthur Alexander, and Berry Gordy), the Stones' covers generally had a bit more bite. Compare Carole King/Gerry Goffin, Burt Bacharach, and Meredith Willson (above) to Willie Dixon, Bo Diddley, and Muddy Waters (below).

the pure sap of "A Taste of Honey," a thoroughly mediocre cover of "Chains," written by Carole King and Gerry Goffin, and a version of Arthur Alexander's "Anna (Go to Him)." None of those does anything for me.

GK: Yeah, it would be easy to say the pros at Abbey Road watered that album down, but it needs to be said that even in their rough and rowdy Hamburg days, the Beatles were including such pop standards as "A Taste of Honey" and "Besame Mucho" in their set lists. George Martin undoubtedly encouraged more such "adult," mainstream fare because he wasn't that impressed with the boys' songwriting early on. In fact, he agreed to work with them not because of their songwriting but because he loved their humor. Remember, he even replaced Ringo on a few of the early tracks as the drummer because it wasn't flying for him as a musical thing yet.

It wasn't until later that the Beatles defined themselves as this super-sophisticated rock-pop group—a group that took pop songwriting to a new level, which is their ultimate legacy.

With the Stones, the sound was there from the start: blues with attitude. Jagger was one of many upstart Brits trying to sing like a black man, and he had a band behind him that sounded appropriately rough around the edges. Now, how to turn that into pop music? The chemistry between Mick and Keith took a little longer to develop than the Lennon and McCartney partnership, but once it did, they were going toe to toe with the Beatles on the pop charts through the mid-Sixties. The Stones' taste in covers had a bit more bite to it. There were no "A Taste of Honey" supper-club covers for them. They were taking another generation's music and selling it to their peers, and it sounded pretty damn exciting.

Tired of being sold, the Beatles affect their best Stones imitations.

The Ed Sullivan Show, New York City, February 9, 1964: the first step in Epstein's U.S. invasion.

JD: If you had never heard Willie Dixon's "I Just Want to Make Love to You" or Chuck Berry's "Carol," it was mind-blowing. If the Stones had never done anything beyond that first album, they'd still have made a contribution by prodding some young listeners to go out and discover Bo Diddley, Willie Dixon, or Chuck Berry on their own. "Okay, these guys and their covers are cool, but what do the originals sound like?"

GK: Which is why Oldham really pushed Jagger and Richards to start writing their own songs. He knew they needed to make their own mark as songwriters. That may have been his single biggest contribution to the band from a musical standpoint.

The Beatles, on the other hand, were very much a pop group from the start, and by the end of 1963, Epstein had already engineered a deal with Ed Sullivan to get the Beatles on the biggest variety show in America. He also engineered a movie deal for them. He was laying the groundwork for the U.S. invasion in the same year that the Beatles debuted. Sullivan happened to be in London in 1963 when the Beatles arrived home after a brief tour of Sweden, the same month they were going to perform for the Queen. Sullivan was asking, "What's all of this hubbub about the Beatles?" He was a gossip columnist, don't forget, which meant he had a nose for news. And the Beatles were news. Sullivan didn't understand the music, necessarily, but he signed these guys, who were still pretty much unknown in America, to a three-appearance deal on his show. He wanted in on the fad before it wore itself out.

The Stones came to America in mid-'64, a few months after the Beatles, and Sullivan wanted nothing to do with them. They got shuffled off to *Dean Martin's Hollywood Palace*, where the host made fun of them. Dino had nothing but contempt for these ingrates. Who were these punks honing in on the Rat Pack's turf?

JD: Well, if you read Nick Tosches' book on Dean Martin, *Dino: High in the Dirty Business of Dreams*, there were more similarities between Martin and Jagger than differences!

Dutch picture sleeve for "Satisfaction," the anthem of consumer manipulation and the first significant example of great Stones songwriting.

"OK, they play cool covers, but what do their originals sound like?" Pushing Jagger and Richards to write their own songs may have been Oldham's single biggest contribution to the band, but it was also the beginning of the end for Jones. The band takes a break at the ABC Theatre in Belfast, January 6, 1965.

GK: How true. But the Stones would soon enough get their shot in the living rooms of America. The first great Jagger-Richards song, "(I Can't Get No) Satisfaction," knocked down the doors. It defined pop radio in 1965. Jagger figured out what he wanted to say lyrically, and they melded those R&B and blues influences with giant hooks. This was a full frontal assault on suburbia and its consumerist values, and it would be a theme on subsequent singles. The Beatles never had an overt agenda in that sense. Their approach was more subtle.

JD: You think so? In 1964, with *Beatles for Sale*, the very title finds the group signaling that they are sick of being marketed, packaged, and sold. They look exhausted and sullen on the cover of their fourth album—kind of like the Stones, actually! It's the first time you see that attitude on a Beatles cover. Meanwhile, the American version of the Stones' *Out of Our Heads*, released in July 1965, not only gives us "Satisfaction," an epic anthem of consumer manipulation and the

first significant example of great Stones songwriting, but it also includes "The Under Assistant West Coast Promotion Man," a song specifically about the salesmanship and manipulation of the music industry. The Stones are sick and tired of being sold, too. It's as if both bands are saying, "Okay, now we understand how the marketing machine works, and we don't want to play that game anymore."

GK: "Revolution" becomes commodity. Happens to everyone! The Stones were frustrated in many ways that their records did not sound as good as the Beatles', despite the presence of people like Glyn Johns as engineer and Jack Nitzsche as jack-of-all-trades instrumentalist. Oldham, ostensibly the "producer," had about as much business being in the studio as Brian Epstein did, but Epstein was smart enough to leave the heavy lifting to George Martin. The Stones had no George Martin in their camp until Jimmy Miller came along as producer for *Beggars Banquet* in 1968.

A DISTINGUISHED HOTEL

The Whittier

Burns Drive • Detroit 14, • Michigan

EXECUTIVE OFFICE

September 6, 1964

TO WHOM IT MAY CONCERN:

This is to certify that the "Beatles" stayed at The Whittier Hotel, arriving at 1:17 A. M. September 6, 1964 (Detroit Time), occupying Executive Suite No. 1566, checking out at 2:05 P. M. September 6, 1964.

This is also to certify the bed linen below so designated is authentic and factual as to each of the "Beatles" using same.

Jimmie Hawkins
Managing Director

GEORGE
SLEPT
HERE

©1964 EINHORN — VICTOR PRODUCTIONS — CHICAGO

THE FABULOUS
BEATLES
JEWELLERY BROOCH

THE FABULOUS
BEATLES
JEWELLERY BROOCH

THE FABULOUS
BEATLES
JEWELLERY BROOCH

THE FABULOUS
BEATLES
JEWELLERY BROOCH

BEATLES
NEW SOUND GUITAR
Made in England under licence

BEATLES
BUBBLES
NEW BEATLES SOAP BUBBLES
8 OZS.

OFFICIAL
TIE TACK PIN

THE BEATLES

BEATLES' HAIR!

SUPPLY IS LIMITED

For that special Beatlemaniac.

Yes BEATLE FANS ... Yesterday our troubles seemed so far away. So come together now and discover what millions have before, that LOVE is all you need! Experience what magic their mop-tops brought to others. Take this card, hold tight and SHAKE!

BELIEVE IT

ACTUALLY contains a lock of hair from one of the Fab Four.

THE HEART OF THE 60's STILL BEATS!

SEALED WITH A KISS!

YEAH!YEAH!YEAH!

HELP! BEATLES HELP!
UNITED ARTISTS 1965

The Rolling Stones, "who haven't bathed in a week," arrive in New York City, June 1964.

JD: I hear what you're saying about the Beatles having a much better sound and the Stones being frustrated by the recording quality. Yet "Satisfaction" is immortal, "The Last Time" is classic, too, and "Play with Fire" is the first sign that these guys have a lot more depth and sophistication and can do more than a blues/rock 'n' roll shuffle. The Stones' choice of covers is stronger as well. They do "Hitch Hike" by Marvin Gaye and "Good Times" by Sam Cooke, and they give more love to Bo Diddley with "I'm All Right." What are the Beatles doing at that point? "Rock and Roll Music" by Chuck Berry—it's obvious and not even one of Berry's best—and "Mr. Moonlight." I still can't believe that Lennon stooped to

sing that! Leiber and Stoller's "Kansas City"—okay, that's a good song. Then there are the Buddy Holly and Carl Perkins covers, which are nothing great. In the end, I think *Out of Our Heads* is a more edgy, dangerous, and sexy album than *Beatles for Sale*.

GK: But the Stones had narrower range. They knew what they loved, and they mined that deep blues/soul vein. The Beatles connected to the universality of someone like Elvis, who explored all sorts of genres, from easy listening to rockabilly, for better or worse. Elvis could take on any style of music and make it his own. The Beatles' early records both benefited and suffered from

out of
  our heads
THE ROLLING
STONES*

Edgier, sexier, more dangerous than *Beatles for Sale*. The U.S. and U.K. sleeves.

out of
our heads uk
THE
ROLLING
STONES*

Despite the Stones' alleged lack of hygiene (or because of it, if you believe Oldham's spin), the band was greeted enthusiastically by American fans.

a similar desire to cover the range of American music, and that broadness made them far more universally loved than the Stones ever would be. There was an element of manufactured rebellion about the Stones: "Would you let your sister go with a Rolling Stone?" That was a headline written by Oldham for *Melody Maker*.

JD: On the other hand, didn't they get busted for pissing on a garage wall?

GK: I'm not saying they weren't bad boys, but Oldham definitely amped it up. When the Stones arrived in New York in 1964, the press release Oldham sent out read,

"The Rolling Stones, who haven't bathed in a week, arrived here yesterday." Can you imagine Epstein writing something like that about the Beatles?

At the same time, there was mutual respect. One of the prevailing myths about the music of the Sixties was that there was an atmosphere of friendly—and sometimes not-so-friendly—competition among the big hitters of the day. Bob Dylan, the Beach Boys, the Byrds, the Stones, the Beatles, the Who, and the Kinks were all watching one another and trying to outdo whatever band was on top at the moment. They made one another better. Do you buy into that?

A police officer plugs his ears while the Beatles perform on their tour of America, September 1964.

Blowing the Stones away with the scope of their sonic invention.

JD: Absolutely, and I think that while I've been favoring the Stones in terms of their image here, just liking it more and liking those first couple of Stones albums more than the Beatles' first few records, the Beatles quickly learned how to use Abbey Road Studios to blow their listeners' minds. They were jumping forward in incredible leaps and bounds. There is schlock on the first couple of Beatles albums, but they were getting somewhere, and they were learning how to use the tools at their disposal, whereas with the Stones, the breakthroughs in sound were coming fewer and farther between. By the time we get to *Help!* and *December's Children (And Everybody's)*—the Beatles hitting the record stores in August 1965 and the Stones that December—the scope of the Beatles' sonic invention is blowing the Stones away. "Help!" is a very inventive track; "You've Got to Hide Your Love Away" doesn't

sound like anything else up to that point, and "Ticket to Ride" has got the drone, the drive, and the mystery of that echo. Even "Yesterday" is amazing. In retrospect, it's easy to scoff at the song the Beatles themselves called "Scrambled Eggs," and after you hear it one time too many in the elevator or at the dentist's office, it starts to drive you crazy, but try to remember the first hundred times you heard it and how powerful it was as a deep romantic ballad. Then there are "Tell Me What You See" and "I've Just Seen a Face," which are pretty sophisticated songs that become even more mysterious thanks to the way they were recorded.

On the other side of the fence, after you get past "Get Off of My Cloud," which is a really impressive jump forward for the Stones in the studio, and to some extent "As Tears Go By" and "I'm Free," the band isn't showing nearly as many new tricks.

Lennon and McCartney take a break from the filming of *Help!* in Obertauern, Austria, March 1965.

Aftermath (above) along with a Japanese EP from 1966 (right) featuring "Satisfaction," "As Tears Go By," "Get Off of My Cloud," and "19th Nervous Breakdown." This period was the cap in the Stones' great singles era.

GK: The Stones were more of a singles band up until *Aftermath* in 1966, the first really great Stones album beginning to end.

JD: *Aftermath* is also the first Stones record on which Jagger and Richards write every song.

GK: Right. It was the album that put the cap on the Stones' great singles era: "Satisfaction," "Get Off of My Cloud," "19th Nervous Breakdown," "Paint It, Black," "Mother's Little Helper," and "Have You Seen Your Mother, Baby, Standing in the Shadow?" Whereas the Beatles had already hit their stride as a great album band in 1965 with *Help!*

JD: Then as *December's Children* is hitting the stores in December 1965, the same week, the Beatles are beating the Stones' ass again in terms of studio sophistication with *Rubber Soul!*

GK: *Help!* is the prelude to all that. They take the British Invasion sound, the Merseybeat sound, as far is it can go. Just listen to that title song again—there isn't a wasted note or an empty gesture. It's a beautiful, economical arrangement that brims with invention, excitement, surprise, and hooks. Lennon hammers the rhythm guitar, Starr's fills goose the excitement, the call-and-response vocals manage to make the singer's desperation sound like a thrill ride. Like, get me off this rollercoaster that my life has become! And then the Beatles follow that up by reinventing themselves with *Rubber Soul*, riffing on Dylan's sound: folk guitars

Folk guitars crossed with rock aggression and more open-ended lyrics.

Beating the Stones' asses again in terms of studio sophistication! The Beatles, that is, not these matronly workers in the EMI factory at Middlesex, England, who are putting the finishing touches on *Rubber Soul* in November 1964 before it's shipped to stores.

crossed with rock aggression, and more elliptical, open-ended lyrics. What really happens in a song like "Norwegian Wood"? We're not sure. There seems to be some kind of illicit affair, and then the narrator sets a fire at the end. Does he burn down his lover's house? You have satire creeping into "Drive My Car," and the lush swoon of a song like "Girl." These were just wonderfully sophisticated pop songs.

JD: The first Stones album to follow *Rubber Soul* was *Aftermath*, and there isn't a single toss-off on that one, either. The Stones really stack the first half of the British version of that album: "Mother's Little Helper," "Stupid Girl," "Lady Jane," "Under My Thumb"—man, that's an impressive roll! But again, it's coming quite a bit later than the Beatles' studio breakthrough, and I think you have to admit that the Stones were running to catch

up with what the Beatles were doing at the recording console. And then they just sort of give up even trying to keep pace not long after *Their Satanic Majesties Request*. After that, I think the Stones decided to be more about attitude and mood and less about innovation in the record studio.

GK: The Stones really had no patience for that sort of thing. Can you imagine Keith Richards manipulating backward tape loops for days at a time? Whereas the Beatles almost over-compensated for their dissatisfaction with live performance by going nuts in the studio. They had great, technically adept accomplices who helped them realize the sounds they heard in their heads. Not just George Martin, but engineers like Geoff Emerick and Norman Smith, who were willing to go wherever they led.

The Beatles, bathed in the virginal light of *The Ed Sullivan Show*, February 4, 1964.

JD: You could argue that the Beatles were all about control in the studio and the Stones were about letting loose and then getting the hell out of there. But we also have to ask the question: Which was the more powerful live band at this point? The Beatles had pulled out of live performances by the time they got to *Revolver* in the later half of 1966, of course, but still, look at the footage from *The Ed Sullivan Show* of both bands. Patti Smith would become a powerful rock 'n' roll force of her own, but before that, she famously wrote of sitting on the floor in her living room with her father on the couch watching the Stones on *Sullivan* and "shooting the first gob of gooey in my virgin panties." I look at the girls who scream when the Beatles are playing and, you know, good ol' Ringo is bouncing up and down and George, John, and Paul move into the choreographed thing

of harmonizing into the mike, and it just strikes me as cute. With the Stones, even though I am a red-blooded, heterosexual male, I've got to say that I understand what Smith was talking about—that electric, sexual thrill that comes from watching the Stones perform.

GK: Sullivan never warmed up to the Stones, but they were so popular he ended up having them on his show several times. I'll never forget as a kid seeing them play "Paint It, Black" on *Sullivan*. The opening sequence is Brian Jones almost completely immersed in shadow playing this exotic instrument, and I had no idea what it was. It turned out to be a sitar, of course.

JD: When he does look up, there is such disdain in his eyes: "You're *lucky* I'm here."

GK: He never broke a smile: "I'm cooler than you'll ever be." The darkness, the drive of Charlie's toms, the drone of that sitar—it was way different than seeing the smiling Beatles in the bright, white light, so clearly thrilled to be there. There's almost a virginal quality to it. There was nothing virginal about the Stones. Jagger's lips should've been thrown in jail!

JD: In the innumerable garage revivals we've seen sweep America and the U.K. in the last couple of decades—first-wave groups like the Fleshtones and the Chesterfield Kings, or later bands like the Miracle Workers and the Vipers in the mid- to late-Eighties— there are countless groups that look at the Stones' TV footage and emulate it in their fashions, instruments, and stage moves, and it all strikes new, young audiences as incredibly cool and thrilling. In contrast, almost anyone who puts on matching suits and leans in cheek to cheek to harmonize into one microphone just really looks square at any point after 1964—and it was sort of cheesy even then.

GK: It's state fair, revival-band time when you see something like that. The history books tell us that the Beatles inspired thousands of garage bands to form the day after they appeared on *Ed Sullivan* for the first time. Roger McGuinn picked up a Rickenbacker guitar because he saw the Beatles use one in *A Hard Day's Night*, but the sound and look of the classic guitar-bass-drums band was forged by the Stones.

FALLIN' THROUGH THE SILVER SCREEN

THE BANDS IN THE MOVIES

by Jim DeRogatis

As I see it, in their primes, the Beatles and the Rolling Stones made one great movie each, though those succeed for reasons that are diametrically opposed. As for the rest of their filmographies . . . well, then there's the rest. (And no, I'm not going to get into the posthumous Beatles flicks or the slew of later-day Stones concert films—Jagger and Richards towering on IMAX screens at age sixty-five is a sight that not even Martin Scorsese could make appealing!)

THE BEST

A HARD DAY'S NIGHT *(1964)*

Above and beyond the fact that it was a brilliant marketing ploy by Brian Epstein at the same time that it satirized the star-making machinery, the Beatles' first film is a wickedly funny Marx Brothers–style comic romp. Director Richard Lester set the template for rock 'n' roll on film—and the video era that followed—with his frenetic pacing and energizing jump cuts. Just try not to get caught up in the excitement.

GIMME SHELTER *(1970)*

Working with Charlotte Zwerin, veteran documentary makers Albert and David Maysles captured the enticing electricity of the Stones as they toured the United States and performed at Altamont in 1969, as well as the callous and/or naïve attitudes they displayed in their removed-from-it-all superstardom, which ultimately resulted in a man being beaten and stabbed to death right before our eyes. It's as harrowing as *A Hard Day's Night* is entertaining. Both are unforgettable.

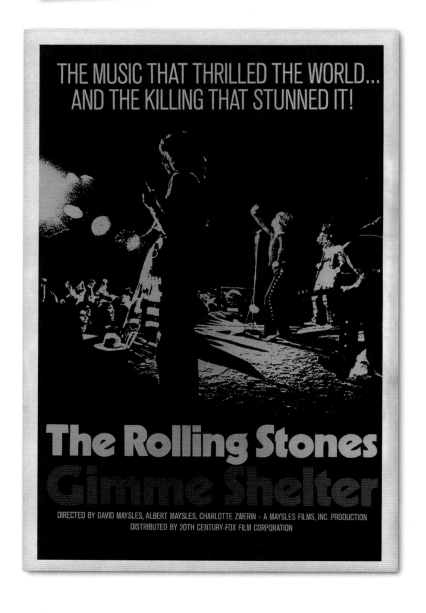

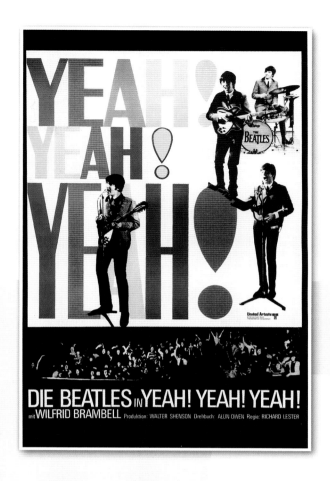

Japanese, West German, French, and Italian posters for *A Hard Day's Night*.

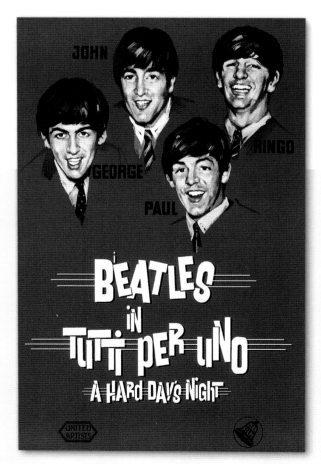

43

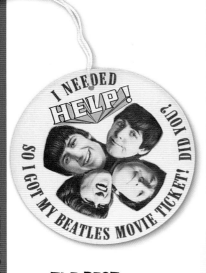

THE REST

HELP! *(1965)*
Sure, we all love the notion of the Beatles living together in one interconnected super-swingin' Space Age bachelor pad, but the group's second feature film is dragged down by its stupid stolen-ring plot, boasting the most cloying aspects of the Bond films but few of the charms.

CHARLIE IS MY DARLING *(1966)*
Shot during a two-day tour of Ireland in September 1965, the first documentary about the Stones really doesn't capture how thrilling they were at the time, and director Peter Whitehead was no Richard Lester.

MAGICAL MYSTERY TOUR *(1967)*
This hour-long made-for-TV mess finds the Beatles donning silly costumes and rolling around the countryside for no discernable reason. This, kids, is why the indiscriminate use of psychedelic drugs really isn't a good idea.

SYMPATHY FOR THE DEVIL *(1968)*
Originally entitled *One Plus One* by renowned French director Jean-Luc Godard, these 110 minutes of the Stones in the recording studio—interspersed with footage of the Black Panthers and other cutting-edge sights of the times—actually seem ten times longer, though if you fast-forward to the parts where "Sympathy for the Devil" evolves through different grooves until it finally gels, those glimpses of inspiration in action are amazing.

YELLOW SUBMARINE *(1968)*
Why the indiscriminate use of psychedelics is a bad idea, part two—though to be fair, the Beatles really didn't have much to do with this turd, appearing only at the end of the film, and not even voicing their own (poorly) animated characters.

THE ROLLING STONES ROCK AND ROLL CIRCUS *(1968)*
The Stones' attempt to bring their act to television was no better than the Beatles', with a cheesy Big Top conceit and appearances by Eric Clapton, John Lennon and Yoko Ono, Jethro Tull, Taj Mahal, and the Who, with the latter upstaging their hosts in a fiery performance. (Recorded early in the morning, the Stones either weren't quite awake or were fading fast from the previous night's excesses.) Never aired as intended by the BBC in the Sixties, it was finally released in 1996, and it proved to have not been worth the wait.

LET IT BE *(1970)*
Aside from the famous Apple rooftop concert, this is pretty much a sad and listless look at the dissolution of one of the best bands of all time.

COCKSUCKER BLUES *(1972)*
This notorious and still officially unreleased piece of cinéma vérité by Robert Frank looms much, much larger in legend than it does on the actual screen. Yeah, Jagger snorts cocaine, hirsute hippies cavort in the nude, roadies go wild, and so on, but it really makes the chaos of the Stones on tour in 1972 seem surprisingly boring.

LADIES AND GENTLEMEN: THE ROLLING STONES *(1974)*
This is more effective than *Cocksucker Blues* as a document of the same '72 tour because it just gives us the Stones onstage at their peak during four shows in Texas. The film was originally hyped for its quadraphonic sound, which must have been pretty impressive in the theaters equipped for it.

Filmmaker Jean-Luc Godard consults with Jagger during the making of *Sympathy for the Devil* as other Stones look on.

Eric Clapton, Lennon, Mitch Mitchell, and Richards— a.k.a., The Dirty Mac—on the set of *Rock and Roll Circus.*

45

2

THE SINGER, NOT THE SONG

THE VOCALISTS

It's about charm, not great singing. Jagger and Richards, Denmark, 1970.

JD: If we're going to set up an *American Idol*–style vocal contest between the Beatles and the Stones, I think it's a no-brainer, right? As the conventional thinking goes, the Beatles could sing like angels, and the Stones barely could sing at all!

GK: The Beatles had a much more sophisticated approach to vocals, especially with the harmonies. They were big fans of the Everly Brothers, big fans of Brill Building pop, the Shirelles, and the Ronettes, and they loved those layered vocals. John Lennon and Paul McCartney individually were great singers, but when you add the counterpoint harmonies on top of that with George Harrison, it's no contest.

Fans of the Everly Brothers, the Brill Building, and the girl groups, the Beatles loved those layered vocals. McCartney, Lennon, and Harrison, 1964.

I don't think Mick Jagger ever aspired to be a great pop singer, though he became one in later decades. He was a shouter and a showman. Keith Richards' backing vocals often sounded like the drunk who had passed out in the alley, stumbled into the recording session, and learned his part as he was singing it. There's a charm there, but it's not about "great" singing. Yet Jagger shouldn't be so easily dismissed. Before words like "postmodern" started showing up in rock reviews, Jagger defined the postmodern attitude. There was a sense of irony and satire in his voice that set him apart from many of his peers, Bob Dylan excepted. He didn't see himself as any kind of poet, but the best Stones songs had two great qualities: anger and dark wit.

Blues aficionado and fan of American roots music Mick Jagger, Olympia Music Hall, Paris, August 20, 1965.

JD: There also is the fact that Jagger was a blues aficionado, a fan of American roots music. As he sang the blues—and, later on, as he sang country—you can hear him imitating his heroes and at the same time laughing at himself for being an upper-middle-class Englishman imitating poor black sharecroppers or poor white hillbillies. I'm thinking of an over-the-top performance like "Shake Your Hips" or, among the country songs, "Dear Doctor." One way to hear those tunes is that he's sneering at those styles and the originators of those sounds, but the other way is that he knows and loves those genres. He knows we expect to hear them with the hillbilly drawl or the sharecropper's slur, and that's what he's going to give us even as he's laughing at himself about doing it.

GK: It's almost like he couldn't take himself seriously in the country songs "Far Away Eyes" or "Dead Flowers." In a way, he was mocking the earnestness of some of his contemporaries who were also adopting these styles. Jagger's take was, "Who are we trying to kid?"

The Stones were the first postmodern blues or roots-rock band. When you think about the blues and country music, you think of this overwhelming sense of sincerity in addressing issues like fear, despair, and sadness, and most rock-era artists are pretty reverent about the way they approach that tradition, whether you were Alexis Korner in Sixties London or Uncle Tupelo in Belleville, Illinois, in the Nineties. The Stones started out mimicking those styles, bringing a mixture of respect and skepticism because they knew it was preposterous

Jagger had the sense to laugh at himself as an upper-middle-class Englishman imitating sharecroppers and hillbillies.

for them to claim they were somehow authentic. They grew up in the London suburbs, which might as well have been Mars as they attempted to appropriate the sounds of the Mississippi Delta. The Stones' version of the "blues" endures because they weren't just mimics. Jagger made it clear early on that, in his view, the "sincerity" of the more earnest British blues guys was a bit much, as well. So why not take it in a more flamboyant direction?

JD: Well, that's subjective. Think of what Robert Plant did with "Bring It on Home" by Led Zeppelin: He was consciously trying to imitate an old black bluesman from the South in the slow parts of the song, and he wasn't laughing at himself about it. I'm a big Zeppelin fan, but it still sounds ludicrous and almost offensive to me. With Jagger, I don't think he ever was really sneering at or condescending to this music. He loved it. He knew he couldn't really sing like a hillbilly or an old black

bluesman, so he was just having fun. But to get back to the key point of what you were saying about attitude, of course, rock 'n' roll is ninety-eight percent attitude. You can't dismiss that rooster strut across the stage or detach it from the vocal performance because it's one and the same! It's a way of putting a song over. People would say Dylan can't sing, and people would say Jagger can't sing, yet could you imagine the Stones with any other vocalist? Would you want Joe Cocker fronting the Rolling Stones? Hell no!

GK: No, absolutely not. Jagger is one of the great rock 'n' roll frontmen in the traditional sense of that term. He didn't really play an instrument, barring the occasional harp solo . . .

JD: And, now that he's old, picking up a guitar every few songs to give himself a break!

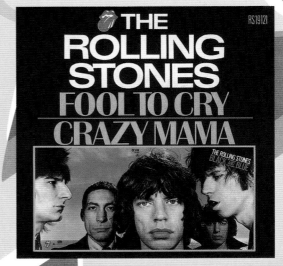

French picture sleeve for "Fool to Cry," a tip of the hat to Smokey Robinson and Philly soul.

Japanese picture sleeve for "Angie." Was the song as honest as Jagger ever got, or utterly insincere? Either way, it's *not* about Angela Bowie.

Jagger transformed "Midnight Rambler" into grand theater on the 1969 U.S. tour, the turning point for the Stones.

GK: But the turning point for the Stones in becoming the biggest band in the world was the '69 tour of America, with Jagger transforming "Midnight Rambler" into grand theater. He inhabited this despicable character. A lot of those songs were acting jobs. He was not attempting to say, "This is me, these are my innermost feelings, and I am wearing my heart on my frilly French sleeve." He was role-playing. In the Seventies, with the band adrift amid drugs and celebrity, he added a new wrinkle:

tenderness. Not exactly a predictable emotional stance for the man who gave us "Stupid Girl" and "Stray Cat Blues" and other bits of black-hearted contempt. But here he was crooning "Angie," "Memory Motel," and "Fool to Cry"—a tip of the hat to Smokey Robinson and Philly soul. Suddenly, Jagger was keeping the Stones on the charts with ballads—yikes! I don't believe a single word he sings in them, but he sells those songs very well. I give him credit for doing whatever it took to keep the Stones rolling.

Did the ubiquity of Stones songs make it hard to hear the brilliance of Jagger's performances?

JD: Really? I don't think it's direct and sweet, but I see "Angie" as probably the most honest song he has ever delivered. Here's this guy who finds the kicks just keep getting harder to find. He's a millionaire who can fulfill any and every whim and indulge in levels of wretched excess that you and I can't even imagine, and in this song—which, contrary to the long-since-debunked rumor, is *not* about Angela Bowie—I think he's realizing that, "Wow, I have everything, and yet I have nothing— no true connection with anybody." And he's doing that by looking at a failed relationship where he did have that: *"With no loving in our souls and no money in our coats/ You can't say we're satisfied."*

GK: You think poor, penniless Mick is pouring out his feelings in that song?

JD: No, but I do think he's feeling sorry for himself, and that's as sincere as he's ever gotten! Poor Mick Jagger,

it's so hard to be a multimillionaire who can revel in any Bacchanalian delight . . . but hey, it's lonely at the top. Just ask Caligula!

GK: Gotta disagree. Jagger at his most sincere? I'll take "(I Can't Get No) Satisfaction." We take that song for granted, we've heard it so much. But it came on the radio the other day, and I listened to it as if it was a new song, and, you know what? It's extraordinary. Of course it is, right? But it just hit me what a masterful performance that is by the then twenty-one-year-old Michael Phillip Jagger. Not just his snarl, his very apparent contempt, but also the intelligence in the lyrics and phrasing, which are well beyond just primitive fist-punching. He's not only sneering at suburbia, but also at the way suburbia is marketed to. It's a very sophisticated statement packed into a seemingly simplistic song. Kurt Cobain would be doing much the same thing twenty-five years later.

Recording "Sympathy for the Devil," Olympic Studios, London, June 1968.

Filming a scene for *Help!*, April 1965.

JD: I still think that when Jagger got to the top and was hanging out with Bianca and Truman Capote and Andy Warhol, some part of him realized how empty it all was. It was a really fleeting moment, perhaps, post-Altamont, and post–*Exile on Main St.* But regardless, what you were saying about the ubiquity of these songs making it hard to hear the brilliance of the performances—that holds true in spades for the Beatles. The construction of those harmonies and group vocals . . . we hear the Beatles singing now, and we just think, "Oh, yeah, that's the Beatles singing again." But if you've ever been in a garage band and tried to cover one of their songs, say, or if you just really listen to and try to dissect the vocal parts—good luck to you! I'm not a musicologist, and plenty of treatises have been written about exactly what the Beatles are doing with the vocal harmonies—triads and all that impressive stuff—but I'm just saying that as a layman who can't really sing himself, if you step back the next time you hear any Beatles track and think about what they're doing vocally, you're going to be blown away.

GK: That vocal interaction certainly impressed the hell out of George Martin. To him, those harmonies suggested a band that could be extraordinary, that could separate themselves from every other boy band with guitars at the time. Individually, they were amazingly strong personalities as well. Lennon the vocalist had all the attitude that Jagger had, and also a scary intensity—the way he could summon rage or sadness. He also had a conversational quality to his voice. In a song like "A Day in the Life," he's weaving these elliptical lyrics into a performance that sounds dreamy and yet as direct as someone talking to you on the couch in your living room. That's pretty tough to pull off. Lennon sang with tremendous conviction, and that's not something that can be readily instilled.

"Oh yeah, that's the Beatles singing again." London Palladium, January 12, 1964.

McCartney, the great vocal stylist, at rehearsal, February 1964.

JD: So there is no contest: The Beatles are better singers than the Stones. We have to grant the Beatles a win in this category. But here's the tricky thing: Who is the better singer in the Beatles? I look at George as a utility singer: He's fine on his own songs and great with the harmony vocals. With Lennon, you have this truly distinctive voice. With McCartney, you have the power: "I Saw Her Standing There" is simply one of the greatest rock vocal performances ever, and if he sang every song like that—and hadn't foisted "When I'm Sixty-Four" and other shticky crap like that on us—I'd have to say he was the man.

GK: "I Saw Her Standing There" is the greatest rock vocal performance in history?

JD: It would be at or near the top on my short list.

GK: I love it, too, but Lennon has it all over McCartney in terms of great vocal performances. On my short list of great Lennon vocals—if you want the sincerity and tenderness in a ballad—"In My Life" is as good as any McCartney ballad. If you want John as a rock 'n' roller, his performance on "Twist and Shout" is amazing, blowing out his vocal cords. If you want the playful avant-garde singer with a dry, sarcastic tinge, "I Am the Walrus" does it for me. That versatility is extraordinary. Then there is Lennon as the mystic in "Strawberry Fields Forever."

With McCartney, he is a great stylist, no doubt about it. He could rock like Little Richard—you listen to "Helter Skelter," and there is a guy tearing his voice out pretty

Lennon as the rock 'n' roll singer, blowing out his vocal cords.

The greatest rock vocal performance ever?

In the vocal category, at least, the Beatles vs. Stones question is an easy one.

convincingly. You want the lullabies? He could do those as well as anyone ever could with songs like "I Will." And there is a great soul singer in there as well, as he demonstrates on "Let It Be." But what really defines McCartney for me is empathy. Listen to "Hey Jude," "Eleanor Rigby," and "She's Leaving Home." Whatever you think about those songs, this is McCartney addressing these characters who aren't like him, aren't even of his generation necessarily, and expressing his regard for how they are handling a particularly stressful situation. And he's doing it with tenderness. When people think back on the Beatles as the "All You Need Is Love" band, the band that embraced the Sixties ideal, that quality shines brightest in McCartney's songs.

JD: The list of great vocal performances from both Lennon and McCartney could go on and on. I would agree with everything you said, and just substitute my favorites in place of yours. I think "Across the Universe" is Lennon in supreme ballad mode, and "Being for the Benefit of Mr. Kite!" is the best Lennon-as-mystic—a tour guide for your acid trip. With Paul, I think "Blackbird" is him at his most tender and winning. Basically, I guess I'm really glad that it's not Lennon vs. McCartney with this book, because with the Beatles vs. the Stones, in the singers' category at least, the answer is easy!

PAPERBACK WRITERS
THE BANDS IN PRINT

by Jim DeRogatis

Hundreds of books have been written about both the Beatles and the Rolling Stones, and while I certainly cannot claim to have read all of them, I believe I've plowed through the most worthy contenders, as well as many of the most hyped. Here are my choices for the best.

THE TRUE ADVENTURES OF THE ROLLING STONES, *by Stanley Booth*

No contest: This is the most artful, most insightful, and just plain best-written book about either band—a work of art that, in its own realm, is every bit as great as the Stones' best albums. Booth rolled with Keith Richards for several years and lived to tell the tale, matching him pill for pill and shot for shot, and sitting atop an amp onstage at Altamont. Novelistic in its scope and construction, this is the rare music book that will thrill a reader even if he or she has never heard a note from the band.

THE COMPLETE BEATLES RECORDING SESSIONS: THE OFFICIAL ABBEY ROAD STUDIO SESSION NOTES, 1962–1970, *by Mark Lewisohn*

While there may be a level of detail that puts off casual fans in what bills itself as "the definitive guide to every recording session done by the Beatles at EMI's Abbey Road recording studio," Lewisohn's exacting tally of how and when the band recorded all of its tunes is fascinating for its nuts-and-bolts revelations. As such, it's become a bible for countless musicians and studio professionals.

THE ROLLING STONES COMPLETE RECORDING SESSIONS, *by Martin Elliott*

Though it isn't nearly as in-depth or as revelatory as the Lewisohn book, Elliott's tome still is valuable for putting the Stones' recording sessions in chronological context. And if there isn't as much detail about what happened at those sessions, well, remember that the Stones were hardly as methodical in, or as enamored of, the recording studio as were the Beatles.

REVOLUTION IN THE HEAD: THE BEATLES' RECORDS AND THE SIXTIES, *by Ian MacDonald*

A musician, composer, and former editor of England's *New Music Express*, MacDonald gamely attempts to place the Beatles' music in the larger context of the myriad political and social movements of the Sixties. His take on things can be a bit Marxist in spots, but it's still a worthy read for anyone looking to understand what they might have missed because they weren't there at the time.

STONE ALONE: THE STORY OF A ROCK 'N' ROLL BAND, *by Bill Wyman with Ray Coleman*

Weighing in at a massive 594 pages in its original hardcover edition, the heft of this autobiographical account by the Stones' bassist is all the more impressive when you realize that it only covers the beginning of the band through the death of Brian Jones in 1969. (I've been waiting for volume two for two decades, but it's still nowhere in sight.) Witty and droll, Wyman can bog down in sometimes tedious detail, but I actually love that trivia. It's a rare thing for any rock legend to recall so vividly every bird he shagged and pound he earned.

THE LIVES OF JOHN LENNON, *by Albert Goldman*

A controversial choice—Beatlemaniacs consider it a hatchet job and slander Goldman as a hack—but, punk that I am, I find that the warts-and-worse revelations about Lennon make his accomplishments all the more remarkable. If a guy this screwed up can make such brilliant art, there may be hope for all of us.

TELL ME WHY: THE BEATLES: ALBUM BY ALBUM, SONG BY SONG, THE SIXTIES AND AFTER, *by Tim Riley*
A DAY IN THE LIFE: THE MUSIC AND ARTISTRY OF THE BEATLES, *by Mark Hertsgaard*

Two books by two music journalists attempting the similar goal of telling the stories behind each of the Beatles' songs, with different but equally enlightening results. Unfortunately, the closest equivalent in the Stones' bibliography, Steve Appleford's *Rolling Stones: Rip This Joint: The Stories Behind Every Song*, doesn't quite measure up.

THE DAY JOHN MET PAUL: AN HOUR-BY-HOUR ACCOUNT OF HOW THE BEATLES BEGAN, *by Jim O'Donnell*

O'Donnell spent eight years researching this labor of love, attempting to construct a minute-by-minute account of the day in 1957 when Lennon and McCartney met, right

two decades after its initial publication, *The Love You Make* stands as the best candidate for a quick-hit overall history of the band if you're reading only one. Brown was one of the suits at the Beatles' management firm and Apple Records, so he had a front-row seat, while Gaines is a solid if rarely flashy journalistic pro.

OLD GODS ALMOST DEAD: THE 40-YEAR ODYSSEY OF THE ROLLING STONES, *by Stephen Davis*

Best choice to fill the same role as *The Love You Make* for the Stones, though with a lot more of the band's post-prime afterlife than we really need (that is, everything post–*Some Girls* into the New Millennium). Alas, it's not nearly as entertaining as Davis' bestselling account of Led Zeppelin, *Hammer of the Gods*.

WHAT WOULD KEITH RICHARDS DO? DAILY AFFIRMATIONS FROM A ROCK 'N' ROLL SURVIVOR, *by Jessica Pallington West*

The very definition of a great bathroom book, this one compiles quotes from the inimitable pirate of rock on topics ranging from Nietzsche to fashion, making a case for Keef as the Zen Buddha of popular music—or at least its Yogi Berra. Witness the sage on the joys of athletic competition: "When I was a junkie, I used to be able to play tennis with Mick, go to the toilet for a quick fix, and still beat him."

down to regular weather reports. He's been knocked by some for inventing some details, and you can weigh my recommendation against the disclosure that he was one of my English teachers at Hudson Catholic Regional School for Boys in Jersey City, New Jersey, back in the early Eighties. But I maintain that this warm and insightful book adds a unique, valuable, and engrossing entry to the library of Beatles literature.

NANKERING WITH THE ROLLING STONES: THE UNTOLD STORY OF THE EARLY DAYS,
by James Phelge

A roommate of Jagger, Richards, and Jones during the early days of the band—and described by Richards as the most disgusting man he ever met, a badge of distinction if ever there was one—Phelge offers a fleeting but nonetheless amusing glimpse of these artists well before their legends were set in stone.

THE LOVE YOU MAKE: AN INSIDER'S STORY OF THE BEATLES, *by Peter Brown and Steven Gaines*

Though some might opt for the more recent *Shout! The Beatles in Their Generation* by Philip Norman, more than

3

NOTHING IS REAL

TWO DIVERGENT PATHS TOWARD THE WHITE LIGHT

JD: When it comes to the psychedelic years, I have to say that it always bugs me that the Beatles are portrayed as the Acid Apostles of the New Age, leading rock 'n' roll into the psychedelic flowering of the mid-Sixties. The Rolling Stones are considered to have sneered at the genre—the drugs, the sounds, and the whole "peace and love" hippie movement—dabbling in it reluctantly, at best, and laughing at it, at worst. Conventional wisdom is that the Stones were mocking *Sgt. Pepper's Lonely Hearts Club Band* with *Their Satanic Majesties Request*, never really buying into

the idea of using psychedelic drugs as the portal to journey "toward the white light," if we want to use the phraseology of the time. I'm going to argue that this view isn't right at all, and that the Beatles and the Stones really got to psychedelia at pretty much the same time, beginning in 1965 and coming to full fruition in 1966.

GK: There are two things to factor in with the Stones. First, Jagger never met a trend that he didn't want to ride. Many may argue that Richards is the rocker who

Written by Jagger for then-girlfriend Marianne Faithfull, "As Tears Go By" makes Top 10 in England.

Sep. 19

Stones release "Time Is on My Side" b/w "Congratulations" in U.S.

Sep. 26

Warren Commission announces Oswald acted alone in Kennedy assassination.

Sep. 27

Free Speech Movement launched at University of California–Berkeley.

Oct. 1

57 escape from East to West Berlin through 475-foot tunnel.

Oct. 3

Beatles record "Eight Days a Week" at Abbey Road.

Oct. 6

Rev. King awarded Nobel Peace Prize.

Oct. 14

Harold Wilson assumes office as prime minister of Great Britain.

Oct. 16

Stones release *12x5* in U.S.

Oct. 17

Michael Ochs Archives/Getty Images

Malcolm X assassinated in front of 400 while speaking in New York City.

Feb. 21

Beatles begin shooting movie *Help!* in Bahamas.

Feb. 22

Stones release first Jagger-Richards-penned U.K. single, "The Last Time" b/w "Play with Fire" in U.K.

Feb. 26

The Sound of Music released.

Mar. 2

State troopers break up march by 600 civil rights demonstrators in Selma, Alabama.

Mar. 7

Robert Abbott Sengstacke/Hulton Archive/Getty Images

Rev. King leads more than 3,000 on 50-mile march from Selma to Montgomery.

Mar. 21

Dylan releases his fifth studio album, *Bringing It All Back Home*, which includes "Subterranean Homesick Blues" and "Mr. Tambourine Man."

Mar. 22

Viola Liuzzo, a white civil rights worker from Detroit, shot and killed by Ku Klux Klan near Selma.

Mar. 25

Pres. Johnson authorizes use of ground troops in Vietnam for combat operations.

Apr. 6

Focus on Sport/Getty Images

Moving into Abbey Road for month-long recording session, Beatles begin work on *Rubber Soul*.

Oct. 12

Orlando Sentinel announces Disney World to be built on 27,000 acres purchased for $5 million.

Oct. 21

Beatles receive MBEs from the Queen at Buckingham Palace.

Oct. 26

Soap opera *Days of Our Lives* premieres on NBC.

Nov. 8

Beatles finish recording *Rubber Soul* with "You Won't See Me" and "Girl," both written at the eleventh hour and each recorded in only two takes.

Nov. 11

Paul Schutzer/Time & Life Pictures/Getty Images

U.S. government sends 90,000 soldiers to Vietnam.

Nov. 14

As many as 25,000 demonstrate in Washington, D.C., against war in Vietnam.

Nov. 27

Stones release *December's Children (and Everybody's)* in U.S. and begin recording *Aftermath* at RCA Studios, Hollywood.

Dec. 4

Michael Ochs Archives/Getty Images

Beatles release *Rubber Soul* and "We Can Work It Out" b/w "Day Tripper" in U.S.

Dec. 6

Beatles release "Paperback Writer" b/w "Rain" in U.S.

May 30

William Masters and Virginia Johnson publish *Human Sexual Response*.

June

Activist James Meredith shot as he walks along a Mississippi highway to encourage black voter registration.

June 6

U.S. Supreme Court issues landmark decision ruling criminal suspects must be informed of constitutional rights prior to questioning by police.

June 13

Beatles release *"Yesterday" ... and Today* in U.S. with its quickly replaced "butcher" cover; Stones release "Mother's Little Helper" b/w "Lady Jane."

June 20

Beatles finish recording *Revolver*, concluding with "She Said She Said."

June 21

Harry Benson/Hulton Archive/Getty Images

Civil rights marchers in Mississippi dispersed with tear gas.

June 23

Betty Friedan and 27 others found National Organization for Women.

June 30

Pres. Johnson signs Freedom of Information Act.

July 4

1962

NASA/Getty Images
John Cohen/Hulton Archive/Getty Images

Pope John XXIII excommunicates Cuban dictator Fidel Castro.
Jan. 3

U.S. sprays pesticide in South Vietnam to reveal whereabouts of Viet Cong.
Jan. 18

British spy Kim Philby defects to U.S.S.R.; Jackie Robinson first African-American elected to Baseball Hall of Fame.
Jan. 23

U.S.S.R. exchanges captured U.S. pilot Francis Gary Powers for Rudolph Abel, a Soviet spy held in U.S.
Feb. 10

Bus boycott starts in Macon, Georgia.
Feb. 12

First Lady Jacqueline Kennedy conducts televised tour of White House.
Feb. 14

Robert Kennedy says U.S. troops to stay in Vietnam until Communism defeated.
Feb. 18

John Glenn first American to orbit Earth.
Feb. 20

Bob Dylan releases his first album on Columbia Records.
Mar. 19

Beatles record at Abbey Road for first time with Ringo.
Sep. 4

U.S. Justice Department files first federal suit to end public school segregation.
Sep. 17

Gov. Ross R. Barnett blocks black student James Meredith from enrolling at University of Mississippi.
Sep. 20

Johnny Carson succeeds Jack Paar as regular host of *The Tonight Show*.
Oct. 1

Beatles release "Love Me Do" b/w "P.S. I Love You" in U.K.
Oct. 5

Pope John XXIII convenes first session of Roman Catholic Church's Twenty-first Ecumenical Council, or Vatican II.
Oct. 11

Pres. Kennedy informed reconnaissance photos reveal long-range missiles in Cuba; Cuban missile crisis begins.
Oct. 16

Pres. Kennedy informs public Cuba has potential to attack U.S. with nuclear warheads.
Oct. 22

U.S. blockade of Cuba begins.
Oct. 24

Keystone/Hulton Archive/Getty Images
Keystone/Hulton Archive/Getty Images

Rev. King begins first nonviolent civil rights campaign in Birmingham, Alabama.
Apr. 2

Lennon's son, Julian, born.
Apr. 8

Winston Churchill made honorary U.S. citizen.
Apr. 9

Beatles release "From Me to You" b/w "Thank You Girl" in U.K.
Apr. 11

Castro arrives in Moscow.
Apr. 27

Andrew Loog Oldham sees Stones perform for the first time.
Apr. 28

Police Commissioner Bull Connor unleashes dogs and firehoses on schoolchildren in Birmingham, Alabama.
May 3

Dylan releases *The Freewheelin' Bob Dylan*, which includes "Blowin' in the Wind," "Masters of War," and "A Hard Rain's a-Gonna Fall."
May 27

Gov. Wallace vows to defy injunction ordering integration of University of Alabama.
June 1

George Freston/Fox Photos/Getty Images
Art Rickerby/Time & Life Pictures/Getty Images
Popperfoto/Getty Images

Stones release cover of Beatles' "I Wanna Be Your Man" b/w "Stoned" in U.K.
Nov. 1

Ngo Dinh Diem and brother assassinated in military coup; *Daily Mirror* coins term *Beatlemania* after reviewing Cheltenham concert.
Nov. 2

Beatles appear at Royal Variety Performance, where Lennon requests, "Will those in the cheaper seats clap your hands? The rest of you can just rattle your jewelry."
Nov. 4

Pres. Kennedy and wife, Jackie, begin two-day tour of Texas.
Nov. 21

With the Beatles released in U.K.; Pres. Kennedy assassinated in Dallas.
Nov. 22

Pres. Lyndon Johnson proclaims Nov. 25 day of national mourning; sci-fi TV series *Doctor Who* debuts in England.
Nov. 23

Millions watch on live TV as Jack Ruby shoots Kennedy's accused assassin, Lee Harvey Oswald, in Dallas.
Nov. 24

Beatles release "I Want to Hold Your Hand" b/w "This Boy" in U.K.; Pres. Johnson appoints Chief Justice Earl Warren head of commission to investigate Kennedy assassination.
Nov. 29

Cronkite airs CBS news report from London on Beatles.
Dec. 10

ENGLAND'S NEWEST HIT MAKERS
THE ROLLING STONES

1964

Beatles record "A Hard Day's Night" at Abbey Road.

Apr. 16

The Rolling Stones released in U.K. (self-titled debut rechristened *England's Newest Hitmakers* for U.S. release on June 13).

Apr. 26

Beatles release "Love Me Do" b/w "P.S. I Love You" in U.S.

Apr. 27

Stones begin recording second album at Regent Sound Studio, London.

May

U.S. Supreme Court rules closing schools to avoid desegregation unconstitutional.

May 25

Stones begin month of recording at Chess Records' house studio, Chicago.

June

Beatles attend Queen Elizabeth's birthday party— at her insistence.

June 11

Stones release "Tell Me" b/w Willie Dixon's "I Just Want to Make Love to You" in U.S.; Civil Rights Act of 1964 survives 83-day filibuster in U.S. Senate and passes by vote of 73–27.

June 19

Stones again move into Chess Records' house studio; Willie Dixon looks on as they record his "Little Red Rooster."

Nov.

John Dominis/Time & Life Pictures/Getty Images

Pres. Johnson soundly defeats Barry Goldwater, winning 61 percent of popular vote.

Nov. 3

Michael Ochs Archives/Getty Images

Comedian Lenny Bruce convicted in New York City on obscenity charges.

Nov. 4

British House of Commons votes to abolish death penalty.

Nov. 9

Stones release "Little Red Rooster" b/w "Off the Hook" in U.K.

Nov. 13

J. Edgar Hoover describes Rev. King as "the most notorious liar in the country" for accusing FBI agents of failing to act on complaints filed by blacks.

Nov. 18

Beatles release "I Feel Fine" b/w "She's a Woman" in U.S.; Vatican abolishes Latin as official language of Roman Catholic liturgy.

Nov. 23

Police arrest more than 800 students at University of California– Berkeley the day after students stage massive sit-in at administration building.

Dec. 3

Beatles record "Help!" at Abbey Road.

Apr. 13

Newscaster Edward R. Murrow dies of cancer.

Apr. 27

Stones begin five months of recording at Chess Records, Chicago, and RCA Studios, Hollywood, producing tracks to appear on *Out of Our Heads* and *December's Children (and Everybody's)*.

May

Warren Buffett takes control of Berkshire-Hathaway, then closing at $18 per share. (In 2006, shares of Berkshire-Hathaway passed $100,000 per share.)

May 10

Stones release "(I Can't Get No) Satisfaction" b/w "The Under Assistant West Coast Promotion Man" in U.S.

May 27

Beatles VI released in U.S.; band records "Yesterday" at Abbey Road.

June 14

Beatles release "Help!" b/w "I'm Down" in U.S.

July 19

Alice Ochs/Michael Ochs Archives/Getty Images

Dylan booed for "going electric" at Newport Folk Festival.

July 25

1966

Bill Ray/Time & Life Pictures/Getty Images

Sam Cooke shot to death by motel manager in L.A.

Dec. 11

Stones release "As Tears Go By" b/w "Gotta Get Away" in U.S.

Dec. 18

Ronald Reagan announces candidacy for California governor.

Jan. 4

Civil rights leader Vernon Dahmer killed in firebombing in Mississippi.

Jan. 10

Pres. Johnson states U.S. should stay in Vietnam until Communist aggression ends.

Jan. 12

Rev. King brings civil rights campaign to Chicago.

Jan. 17

80,000 U.S. soldiers land in Vietnam, bringing total to 190,000.

Jan. 18

Stones release "19th Nervous Breakdown" b/w "As Tears Go By" in U.K.

Feb. 4

July — Pres. Kennedy installs taping system in White House.

July 10 — Rev. Martin Luther King Jr. arrested during demonstration in Georgia.

July 11 — Cosmonaut Andrian Micolaev sets longevity record for manned space flight: four days.

July 21 — 160 civil rights activists jailed after demonstration in Albany, Georgia.

July 27 — Rev. King jailed, Albany, Georgia.

Aug. 5 — Marilyn Monroe found dead in L.A. home—"probable suicide" from overdose of sleeping pills; Nelson Mandela arrested for incitement and illegally leaving South Africa.

Aug. 15 — Lennon and McCartney invite Ringo Starr to join Beatles.

Aug. 16 — Drummer Pete Best fired from Beatles.

1963

Jan. 14 — George Wallace sworn in as governor of Alabama, vowing "Segregation forever!"

Jan. 16 — Khrushchev claims U.S.S.R. has 100-megaton nuclear bomb.

Jan. 17 — Khrushchev visits Berlin Wall.

Feb. 11 — American poet Sylvia Plath commits suicide by gas in London.

Feb. 20 — Beatles record "Misery" and "Baby It's You" at Abbey Road.

Feb. 25 — Betty Friedan publishes *The Feminine Mystique.*

Mar. 18 — U.S. Supreme Court rules poor defendants have constitutional right to attorney.

Mar. 22 — British Minister of War John Profumo denies having had sex with Christine Keeler, a model who was sleeping with Soviet attaché; Beatles release their first album, *Please Please Me*, in U.K.

July 30 — British spy Kim Philby discovered living in Moscow.

Aug. 23 — Beatles release "She Loves You" b/w "I'll Get You" in U.K. (U.S. release follows on Sept. 16).

Aug. 28 — Rev. King delivers "I Have a Dream" speech before Lincoln Memorial, Washington, D.C.

Sep. 2 — Gov. Wallace uses state troopers to prevent integration of Tuskegee High School.

Sep. 9 — Gov. Wallace served with federal injunction ordering him to stop barring black students from enrolling in white schools.

Sep. 15 — Ku Klux Klan bombs 16th Street Baptist Church, Birmingham, Alabama. Four young black girls killed as they prepare Sunday school lesson on "the love that forgives."

Oct. 17 — Beatles record "I Want to Hold Your Hand" at Abbey Road.

Oct. 22 — 225,000 students boycott Chicago schools during Freedom Day protest.

Feb. 9 — Beatles perform on *The Ed Sullivan Show* for TV audience estimated at 73 million.

Feb. 21 — Stones release "Not Fade Away" (a Buddy Holly cover) b/w "Little by Little" in U.K.

Feb. 25 — Cassius Clay defeats heavily favored Sonny Liston to become heavyweight champion.

Mar. 2 — Beatles release "Twist and Shout" b/w "There's a Place" in U.S.; begin filming *A Hard Day's Night* in U.K.

Mar. 9 — First Ford Mustang rolls off assembly line in Detroit.

Mar. 16 — Beatles release "Can't Buy Me Love" b/w "You Can't Do That" in U.S.

Mar. 23 — Beatles release "Do You Want to Know a Secret" b/w "Thank You Girl" in U.S.

Apr. 4 — Beatles hold top five spots on *Billboard* singles chart.

CBS Photo Archive/Hulton Archive/ Getty Images

Bay of Pigs invaders sentenced to 30 years imprisonment in Cuba.

Apr. 8

Walter Cronkite becomes anchorman of *CBS Evening News*.

Apr. 16

Helen Gurley Brown publishes *Sex and the Single Girl*.

May

Brian Epstein meets George Martin; Beatles offered recording contract contingent on results of June 6 recording session.

May 9

U.S. sends troops to Thailand.

May 11

Yale Joel/Time & Life Pictures/ Getty Images

Marilyn Monroe sings "Happy Birthday" to Pres. Kennedy at Madison Square Garden, New York City.

May 19

Nazi war criminal Adolph Eichmann hanged near Tel Aviv for role in murders of more than 1 million Jews.

May 31

Beatles record at Abbey Road Studios, London, for first time, performing "Bésame Mucho," "Love Me Do," "P.S. I Love You," and "Ask Me Why."

June 6

U.S. Supreme Court rules use of unofficial non-denominational prayer in New York public schools unconstitutional.

June 25

Soviet leader Nikita Khrushchev offers to withdraw missiles from Cuba if U.S. closes missile bases in Turkey.

Oct. 26

Pres. Kennedy reports Soviet missile bases in Cuba being dismantled.

Nov. 2

Richard Nixon, who failed in bid to become governor of California, states, "You won't have Nixon to kick around anymore."

Nov. 17

Pres. Kennedy bars religious and racial discrimination in federally funded housing; U.S.S.R. agrees to remove bombs from Cuba; U.S. lifts blockade.

Nov. 20

Great Britain performs nuclear test at Nevada test site.

Dec. 7

Central Press/Hulton Archive/ Getty Images

Lawrence of Arabia released in U.S.

Dec. 16

Accord between U.S. and Cuba wins release of Bay of Pigs captives.

Dec. 21

Eight people in armor-plated vehicle escape East Berlin, crashing through Berlin Wall.

Dec. 26

Beatles release "Please Please Me" b/w "Ask Me Why" in U.K. (release of U.S. single follows on Feb. 25).

Jan. 11

Stones release "Come On" (a Chuck Berry cover) b/w "I Want to Be Loved" (a Willie Dixon cover) in U.K.

June 7

Rev. King arrested in Florida for trying to integrate restaurants; federal troops mobilized to force Wallace to accept two black students at University of Alabama; Buddhist monk Quang Duc immolates himself on Saigon.

June 11

Cleopatra premieres in New York; NAACP leader Medgar Evers fatally shot in front of his home in Jackson, Mississippi.

June 12

U.S. Supreme Court strikes down rules requiring recitation of Lord's Prayer or reading of Bible verses in public schools.

June 17

Pres. Kennedy visits West Berlin, declares "*Ich bin ein Berliner*."

June 26

Myra Hindley and boyfriend Ian Brady, the "Moors Murderers," begin abducting, molesting, killing children in Britain; deadly spree lasts until their arrests in Oct. 1965.

July

Beatles record "She Loves You" at Abbey Road.

July 1

U.S. bans monetary transactions with Cuba.

July 8

Introducing the Beatles released in U.S.

July 22

1964

New York Daily News/Getty Images

Berlin Wall opened for first time; West Berliners allowed one-day holiday visits to relatives in East sector.

Dec. 20

Beatles release "I Want to Hold Your Hand" b/w "I Saw Her Standing There" in U.S.

Dec. 26

Stones begin working on first album at IBC Studios, London.

Jan.

Pres. Johnson declares "War on Poverty" in State of the Union address.

Jan. 8

Plans unveiled for World Trade Center in New York City.

Jan. 18

Meet the Beatles! released in U.S.

Jan. 20

Beatles release "Please Please Me" b/w "From Me to You" in U.S.

Jan. 30

U.S. report entitled "Smoking & Health" links cigarettes to lung cancer.

Jan. 31

Beatles arrive at New York's JFK Airport; Baskin-Robbins introduces Beatle Nut ice cream (pistachio with a chocolate ribbon and walnuts).

Feb. 7

Album *A Hard Day's Night* released by Beatles in U.S.; Stones release "It's All Over Now" b/w "Good Times, Bad Times" in U.K.

June 26

The film *A Hard Day's Night* premieres at Odeon Cinema, Liverpool.

July 10

Beatles release *Something New* in U.S.

July 20

James Bond creator Ian Fleming dies, age 56.

Aug. 12

Chicago suburb of Dixmoor rocked by race riot.

Aug. 15

Beatles release "Matchbox" (a Carl Perkins cover) b/w "Slow Down" in U.S.

Aug. 24

Walt Disney's *Mary Poppins* released.

Aug. 29

Pres. Johnson signs Wilderness Act, designating 9 million acres "where the Earth and its community of life are untrammeled by man."

Sep. 3

Officials at University of California–Berkeley announce new policy prohibiting political action at campus entrance.

Sep. 14

1965

Beatles for Sale released in U.K.

Dec. 4

University of California Academic Senate passes resolutions affirming rights of students to participate in political activities.

Dec. 8

Beatles '65 released in U.S.

Dec. 15

Stones release "Heart of Stone" b/w "What a Shame" in U.S.

Dec. 19

My Fair Lady released in U.S.

Dec. 25

Rev. King defies Alabama injunction against gatherings sponsored by civil rights groups.

Jan. 2

Churchill dies in London, age 90.

Jan. 24

The Rolling Stones No. 2 released in U.K.

Jan. 30

Beatles release "Eight Days a Week" b/w "I Don't Want to Spoil the Party" in U.S., record "Ticket to Ride," "Another Girl," and "I Need You" at Abbey Road.

Feb. 15

Pres. Johnson signs Medicare into law.

July 30

Rioting and looting break out in Watts section of L.A.

Aug. 11

Help! LP released in U.S.

Aug. 13

Beatles play to 55,000 fans at Shea Stadium, New York City.

Aug. 15

Dylan releases *Highway 61 Revisited*, which includes "Like a Rolling Stone."

Aug. 30

Beatles release "Yesterday" b/w "Act Naturally" in U.S.

Sep. 13

Stones release *Out of Our Heads* in U.K.

Sep. 24

Stones release "Get Off of My Cloud" b/w "I'm Free" in U.S.; Truman Capote begins publication of *In Cold Blood* as four-part serial in the *New Yorker*.

Sep. 25

L.A. Dodgers' Sandy Koufax refuses to pitch Game 1 of World Series in observance of Yom Kippur.

Oct. 6

Beatles release "Nowhere Man" b/w "What Goes On" in U.S.

Feb. 21

Lennon tells *London Evening Standard* Beatles are "more popular than Jesus."

Mar. 4

Jacqueline Susann publishes *Valley of the Dolls*.

Apr.

Beatles begin recording *Revolver* at Abbey Road, starting with "Tomorrow Never Knows."

Apr. 6

Stones release *Aftermath* in U.K.

Apr. 15

U.S. troop total in Vietnam reaches 250,000.

Apr. 29

The Church of Satan is formed by Anton LaVey in San Francisco.

Apr. 30

Stones release "Paint It, Black" b/w "Stupid Girl" in U.S.

May 7

Beach Boys release orchestral-pop masterpiece *Pet Sounds*; Dylan releases double album *Blonde on Blonde*.

May 16

Jones, with sitar in foreground, at a Stones TV appearance, 1966. The bluesiest of blues purists steered Jagger and Richards toward psychedelic sounds from 1965 to 1966, helping to keep the band on the pop charts.

keeps the Stones sounding like the Stones, which I think is an exaggerated stance as well, but Jagger is happy to dabble in disco, funk, reggae, techno, psychedelia—whatever flavors are out there selling, he'll try to adapt the Stones' template to fit them. So, psychedelia—why not? Second is the underrated role played by Brian Jones. Many remember him as being the purest of the blues purists among the Stones, at least initially, but he was also the guy visiting Morocco to study and record the Master Musicians of Joujouka. During the Stones' middle period of roughly 1965 through 1967, Brian

Jones' influence on those records was profound in the way he was able to bring in all these exotic instruments and help Jagger and Richards turn this blues-rock band into a Swinging London pop group—edgy and nasty, sure, but still a force on the pop charts with distinctive-sounding singles. A lot of these instruments, most of them played by Jones, influenced the psychedelic sound that you're talking about: dulcimer, sitar, marimba, recorder, oboe, Mellotron. Those voicings added a lot of color to those records, way beyond the Stones' guitar-bass-drums foundation.

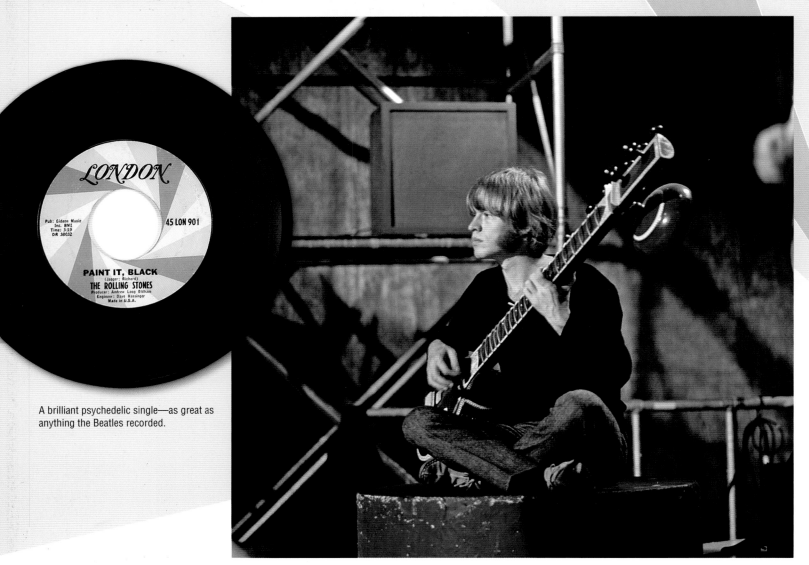

A brilliant psychedelic single—as great as anything the Beatles recorded.

Jones sat for hours learning the sitar. The band recorded "Paint It, Black," and he never recorded with it again.

JD: In my history of psychedelic rock, *Turn on Your Mind*, I argue that while many bands began to make psychedelic rock after experiencing the drugs, just as many avoided the drugs and took inspiration instead from the technological advances in the recording studio and the spirit of experimentation that those fostered. We all know about the Beatles' dalliances with psychedelics, but by all accounts, the Stones were taking the drugs too. Jagger apparently had his first acid experience at a party that was hosted by the Moody Blues, as reported in a story in February 1967 in the *News of the World*. Jagger wasn't quiet about praising LSD: He told his buddy, fashion designer Cecil Beaton, that with LSD, you "see yourself aglow, you see yourself beautiful and ugly and other people as if for the first time." The irony there is that Jagger, forever the mysterious enigma wanting to cloak himself in unanswered questions, actually sued the *News of the World* for libel! Then, a week later, "the Man" got even.

Some people suggest that the *News of the World* called the cops, and that was why Keith's country estate at Redlands was raided. It was considered a setup. Jagger's girlfriend, Marianne Faithfull, was there, prompting the infamous Mars Bar incident (see page 118); also present were gallery owner Robert Fraser and a mysterious American nicknamed "Acid King David," though George and Pattie Harrison ducked out just in time. So in no way were the Stones unfamiliar with taking LSD. By some accounts, Jones got there first in 1965, and by 1966, he was coming on strong, adding those exotic instrumental textures; the music was shifting from black and white to Technicolor. Charlie Watts told the story that Brian Jones sat for hours trying to learn how to play the sitar; the band recorded it for "Paint It, Black," and then Jones never played it again!

"Paint It, Black" is a brilliant psychedelic single—as great as anything the Beatles recorded. The same is true of "19th Nervous Breakdown" and "Mother's

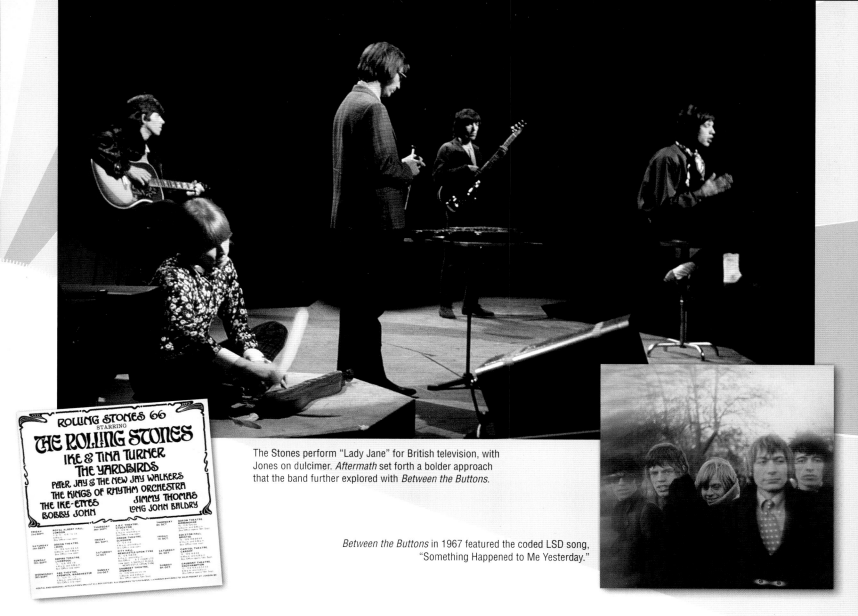

The Stones perform "Lady Jane" for British television, with Jones on dulcimer. *Aftermath* set forth a bolder approach that the band further explored with *Between the Buttons*.

Between the Buttons in 1967 featured the coded LSD song, "Something Happened to Me Yesterday."

Little Helper," though those songs are about speed, not psychedelics. The 1966 best-of compilation, *Big Hits (High Tide and Green Grass)*, showed the band looking entirely stoned; certainly the double entendre of the title wasn't entirely coincidental. But the "Dean of American Rock Critics," Robert Christgau, argued that the Stones made their ultimate comment on LSD with their next album, *Between the Buttons*, in 1967, on the song "Something Happened to Me Yesterday." It's essentially a jug-band ditty of the sort the Grateful Dead were playing before they really found their footing, but Christgau called it "the most accurate LSD song ever." The lyric *"He's not sure just what it was/Or if it's against the law"* is a pretty good summation of the confusion and disorientation of the acid experience.

GK: It's their version of "Ballad of a Thin Man" and Dylan's mocking accusation, *"Because something is happening here/But you don't know what it is/Do you, Mister Jones?"* They're looking at this cop and saying, "You don't have a clue." They're singing in coded language for the people who did turn on, and everyone else was left out in the cold, like poor old Mr. Jones. Speaking of Jones—Brian, that is—he's the one bringing Dixieland flavors to "Something Happened to Me Yesterday." The single was still king, and Jagger wanted to keep up with these pop groups that were storming the charts, whether it was the Zombies or the Who or the Beatles. You look at the difference between the 1965 album *Out of Our Heads* and *Aftermath* the following year, and it's a bolder, more experimental approach, with the Stones really stretching as a band and as songwriters. *Between the Buttons* continues that trend in early 1967, and then the Stones finish off the run with *Their Satanic Majesties Request*. Taken in the context of those previous albums, *Satanic Majesties* is not as big a departure as some would believe.

Lennon and Harrison first tripped in 1964—while at dinner with a dentist.
By most accounts it was a miserable experience, though not because of the dentist.

JD: I don't understand why this period of the Stones is so often overlooked, whereas most hardcore Beatles aficionados will say the stretch that includes *Rubber Soul*, *Revolver*, and *Sgt. Pepper's Lonely Hearts Club Band* represents the band at its best. There is no similar recognition for the Stones in the same era, even though I think the two bands were running neck and neck. The Beatles turning on has been documented more thoroughly than the Stones, in part because the Stones like to play with that mystery. Harrison and Lennon first tripped together in 1964 when they were having dinner with a London dentist. There was a character named Michael Hollingshead who essentially was the Johnny Appleseed of LSD. He traveled around with a mayonnaise jar full of acid that had come from the Sandoz laboratories in Switzerland, where LSD-25 first was synthesized by chemist Albert Hofmann.

Hollingshead saw it as his lot in life to turn on everyone he could, but Harrison and Lennon were miserable throughout that first trip. They ended up speeding around London in Harrison's car, completely freaking out. It wasn't until more than a year later, following Tim Leary's advice in his rewrite of *The Tibetan Book of the Dead* as *The Psychedelic Experience*—all that stuff about controlling set and setting—that Lennon tripped in his attic, journeyed toward the white light, and the next morning gave the band "Tomorrow Never Knows."

GK: "Tomorrow Never Knows" is the absolute peak of that period in more ways than one. To draw a straight line back to that first acid trip you're talking about, I don't think it is coincidental that "Ticket to Ride" came out in early 1965 after the Beatles first started dabbling in psychedelics. The song is a real turning point: the

The Beatles on the set of a promotional film for "Rain" in 1966. The band had begun to use the studio as an instrument for relating the psychedelic experience.

heaviness of Ringo's drums; the drone in the guitar; the laid-back tone of Lennon's voice, as though he's tripping. I don't think there is any coincidence, as well, that this is the first Beatles song to go over three minutes. The texture of the music is changing, it's getting heavier, and the drone is now as important as the melody.

JD: Sonically, that's the key. A lot of critics focus on the lyrics on *Rubber Soul*, saying the Beatles are starting to show an obvious Bob Dylan influence in songs such as "I'm Looking Through You," "Norwegian Wood," and "In My Life." That might be true, but there also is a sonic shift happening. *Rubber Soul* is the beginning of the psychedelic trip, and the bridge is the single "Day Tripper" backed with "Paperback Writer." Then, the use of echo and the beginning of the studio as an instrument in and of itself really flowers with the next single, "Rain,"

which finds Lennon echoing the acid philosopher Alan Watts: "Can we really prove that the sun is shining or if it's raining outside?" The Beatles at this time are playing with slowing down the tapes and using lots of echo and reverb. With the acid experience, people talk about the sense of synesthesia, where you begin to see sound as colors, and that's what's happening in the Beatles' music. I'm neither confirming nor denying my own psychedelic experiences, mind you, but there are certain tonalities resonant of the way you hear the world when you're tripping! I don't think it's a coincidence that you can go back to ancient forms of music like Indonesian gamelan ensembles or Eastern drones and find these sounds that evoke a state of contemplation, meditation, and spiritual transcendence. The Beatles were getting into that hot and heavy in late 1965, and then it exploded in 1966 with *Revolver*.

A true group effort lacking self-consciousness but brimming with experimentation.

Lennon and McCartney work on the collaborative painting *Four Images of a Woman* while on tour in Japan in 1966, just days after beginning the recording of *Revolver*.

GK: Part of *Revolver*'s enduring charm is that even though they were becoming these studiophiles—and, after *Revolver*, they would famously become the non-touring Beatles—there was still a lack of self-consciousness on that record, which would not be the case with *Sgt. Pepper's* a year later. *Sgt. Pepper's* is inevitably hailed as the greatest album of all time, in part because it's considered the official start of the album era, the moment when rock was finally taken seriously by the mainstream media. That may be true, but the music was better on *Revolver*. "Tomorrow Never Knows" is a true group collaboration. It's Lennon's vision, but McCartney completed it by going home and coming up with those five tape loops that ended up being a key part of the song. He taped himself laughing so that it would sound like seagulls, played the sitar and Mellotron, and added all those weird colors that

sonically mirrored Lennon's acid trip. Some musical experts suggest that the drone hadn't been an important factor in Western music since the twelfth century, but here were the Beatles making it an essential part of one of their greatest songs. In 1966, it all seemed fresh, and the psychedelic experience was sparking all sorts of great music. By 1967, with the Summer of Love, it had already become . . .

JD: A marketing ploy! Because I love to deflate myths at every chance, I can't help but insert that Harrison's great awakening to Indian music, according to the most accurate of his biographers, was pure happenstance. There was a guy in the background of a scene when the band was filming *Help!* who happened to be playing sitar. It wasn't like, "The Maharishi came down and opened the skies." It was like, "Hey, what is the weird

In 1966, it all seemed fresh. By 1967, psychedelia had already become a marketing ploy, as this forty-foot in-progress mural on the Beatles' Apple boutique in London seems to confirm.

thing that guy over there is playing?" I love that. These were hungry, open-minded musicians, and I think the Beatles and Stones both were taking in everything and anything that they could at this point. Part of it was artistic experimentation, but part of it also was that they were in competition with each other and everyone else, trying to see who could use the recording studio with the most creativity. They were asking, "What else can we do to distinguish ourselves, to sound different, and to avoid becoming yesterday's news, like Herman's Hermits?" It was a great period, and it worked on every level. In many ways, the argument could end right here, because frankly, as brilliant as they are, the Rolling Stones never made a single album as great as *Revolver*. I have to say it's the best album that either of these bands made. True or false?

GK: Wow. You're wrong. I would put three or four Stones albums—*Exile on Main St.*, *Let It Bleed*, *Sticky Fingers*, *Beggars Banquet*—right alongside *Revolver*. But I *would* say, indisputably, that *Revolver* is the best Beatles album, with *Rubber Soul* and *Abbey Road* following closely behind.

JD: Well, I've had half a lifetime to think about this. If I was forced to bring only one album from either of these groups to a desert island, it would be *Revolver*.

GK: There isn't a weak track on the album, no doubt about that. It is experimental, groundbreaking, radical, avant garde in spots, and yet it is also a great pop album. It has major contributions by all four members. But is it really indisputably better than *Exile on Main St.* or *Let It Bleed*? No way.

SUS MAJESTADES SATANICAS
LOS ROLLING STONES

We love you   Dandelion

PAINT IT, BLACK
THE ROLLING STONES

LONDON   45-901

THE STONES

DECCA

シズ・ア・レインボー
SHE'S A RAINBOW

45r.p.m.
TOP-1240

2000光年の
かなたに
2,000 LIGHT YEARS FROM HOME

ローリング・ストーンズ

シズ・ア・レインボー
2,000 LIGHT YEARS FROM HOME

45r.p.m.
TOP-1240

2000光年のかなたに

THE ROLLING STONES
ローリング・ストーンズ

The Rolling Stones

SHE'S A RAINBOW   2,000 LIGHT YEARS FROM HOME
(Lei e' un arcobaleno)   (2.000 anni luce da casa)

DECCA
F22706

Satanic Majesties was said to be an album made "under the influence of bail," in reference to a drug bust earlier that year at Richards' estate. By late July 1967, with recording still eight weeks from wrapping, the verdict was in. McCartney, seen here with then girlfriend Jane Asher, got the news after returning to London from a vacation in Greece.

Ad for the single purported to express appreciation to Stones fans who supported Richards and Jagger during their legal troubles in the summer of 1967. "We Love You" featured background vocals from Lennon and McCartney.

JD: Sticking to the desert island game, I wouldn't want to be stuck on a desert island with *Exile*, even though I love it, because if that's all I had, I might slit my wrists! It may be the second-best album of all time, but it isn't one you can listen to all the time or exclusively. In any event, now I'm going to say something even more controversial—though it's something I really mean—and that is, *Their Satanic Majesties Request* is a better album than *Sgt. Pepper's Lonely Hearts Club Band*.

GK: Having just listened to *Satanic Majesties* again, I'd have to say you're nuts. *Satanic Majesties* includes some god-awful music. "Sing This All Together (See What Happens)," "Gomper," "2000 Man"—those are pretty

flimsy tracks, and way more self-indulgent than anything on *Sgt. Pepper's*. The Stones were a distracted band at the time. When they were making this record, Jagger, Richards, and Jones all had drug busts hanging over their heads, and they sound like they couldn't bother to actually finish some songs.

JD: The band's famous line was that the album was made "under the influence of bail."

GK: Other people in the Stones camp had to step up.

JD: Bill Wyman did more than he had ever done in the studio at that point.

Inevitably hailed as the greatest LP of all-time, in part because it ushered rock from the singles era to the album era.

McCartney conducts a forty-one-piece orchestra at Abbey Road during the recording of *Sgt. Pepper's*.

GK: And Nicky Hopkins was a big part as well on keyboards.

JD: Absolutely. But even if the lesser moments are not A-level Stones songs—"On with the Show" could be dismissed as hokey vaudeville, "Sing This All Together" is basically an acid campfire song, and Wyman's contribution of "In Another Land" is evidence of why he doesn't have more song credits on Stones albums—they are less offensive than "When I'm Sixty-Four" or "Lovely Rita" or the weaker moments on *Sgt. Pepper's*. Here we are at the epicenter of the youth-culture revolt, the high moment of "tune in, turn on, drop out," and McCartney is romanticizing being

an old geezer and giving us a love song to a cop! And it doesn't end there. With "Getting Better," he talks about beating his woman, and in "She's Leaving Home," he sympathizes with Mom and Dad rather than the girl who's setting off on her own in the first full blush of independence. Again and again, McCartney sympathizes with the establishment on *Sgt. Pepper's* rather the counterculture. Meanwhile, Lennon is tripping like a wildebeest, writing one brilliant song about a circus poster—"Being for the Benefit of Mr. Kite!"—and another, "Lucy in the Sky with Diamonds," full of hallucinatory images and bearing the convenient initials L-S-D. Otherwise, he's pretty much missing in action.

There's an all-inclusiveness to the Beatles' psychedelia that the Stones actively resisted. The band prepares at Abbey Road for the *Our World* live television show, which broadcast to twenty-four countries on June 25, 1967. The band performed "All You Need Is Love" with help from Eric Clapton, Graham Nash, and the Stones.

Not to say everyone bought into the Fab Four's invitation to peace and love. This tract published in 1969 denounced the band as drug-addled sex fiends—and, perhaps worst of all, Communists.

GK: "A Day in the Life" is a great song, too. But to comment on what you're saying about sympathizing with the older generation, when I was talking about the self-consciousness on this album, that was part of it. There is an inclusiveness to the Beatles' psychedelia that the Stones actively resisted. The Stones were still saying "Kiss off" on *Their Satanic Majesties Request*: "Stay away, you don't understand and never will." In fact, they were booting out their manager and producer Andrew Loog Oldham as they were making that album too, because he didn't understand it or want to be any part of it either. The Beatles' vision of psychedelia was partially tongue-in-cheek with "When I'm Sixty-Four," but there was also a sense of "There's room for everyone."

JD: You can't discount the British class system. There was a side to McCartney, as there was to many of the progressive rockers who got their start after *Sgt. Pepper's*, that found him very much wanting to be recognized as a capital-A "Artiste," because it wasn't enough to be a grimy, working-class rock 'n' roller. Many of the British rockers inspired by *Sgt. Pepper's* came from art schools, and they wanted to make their parents proud. You get no sense of that from the Stones. In many ways, it's a much more American attitude.

We could argue forever, but at the end of the day, the Beatles put on the old-time costumes of a Victorian band that might play in the park on Sunday afternoons to make old ladies smile. It doesn't seem like a brave new vision of the future, whereas the cover of *Satanic Majesties* shows the Stones dressed as warlocks, with the threat of dark, dangerous sex magick brewing, as Aleister Crowley might say.

No matter how hard they tried, the Stones couldn't pull off the peace/love/psychedelic trip with straight faces.

Manager Andrew Loog Oldham, background, watches his charges lose the plot during a *Satanic Majesties* session. Before 1967 was over, Oldham would be gone.

GK: Shtick, I say. But there was no lack of shtick in the *Pepper's*-era Beatles either, as they created an alter-ego band and played dress-up on the album cover. If you talk about the blockbuster era when artists like Michael Jackson, Fleetwood Mac, and Bruce Springsteen were trying to make albums that fit every radio format, in some ways, it starts with *Sgt. Pepper's*. The Beatles knew they were the biggest rock band in the world, and they made this open-hearted, universal rock record. By playing to the middle, seeking the widest audience possible, they naturally diluted some of what made them great. *Satanic Majesties* is getting a second wind forty years later because even though it was doing a bit of trend-riding, it did it in a perverse way. It now looks like the more daring record.

JD: Remember that in the chorus of "In Another Land," which Wyman originally entitled "Acid in the Grass," Jagger sings with a sneer, *"Then I awoke/Is this some kind of joke?"* They are laughing the whole way through! And let's not even get into "She's a Rainbow," which probably is the only song in rock history about oral sex with a woman who's having her period. Bottom line: No matter how hard they try, the Stones just can't pull off the peace-love trip with a straight face.

GK: Listen to "2000 Man," where Jagger sings about what he's going to be like in the year 2000: *"Oh, daddy, your brain's still flashin'/Like it did when you were young."* He was doing it as a snide joke then, but here he is, the 2000 man, still at it.

The Stones, shown here in 1968, did not completely turn away from psychedelia after the failure of *Satanic Majesties*, retaining touches of the genre from then on.

JD: Contrary to some accounts, the Stones did not completely turn away from psychedelia after *Satanic Majesties*, even though it was flop and roundly panned by the critics. Even Ian Stewart, the most faithful of Stones sidemen, called it "that damn *Satanic Majesties* album." But echoes of the psychedelic Stones continue with "Child of the Moon," which follows *Satanic Majesties* and is a gorgeous and incredible song. There's also the breakdown in the middle of "Rocks Off" on *Exile on Main St.*, which is pure psychedelia . . .

GK: And "Moonlight Mile" too—a beautiful song that talks about, and sounds like, it was done under a "head full of snow." They did take bits of that legacy and sprinkle it throughout their music. A lot of people think that they took that hard turn on *Beggars Banquet* in 1968, back toward a more linear rock style, because of the utter failure of *Satanic Majesties*, but they retained touches of psychedelia from then on.

It's also interesting where the Beatles went after *Sgt. Pepper's*. Lennon was fed up with the gimmickry and spending nine months in the studio to make a record. You listen to a song like "I Am the Walrus," and it certainly is psychedelia incarnate, but he's taking the piss out of the whole era in a way. It is a big middle finger to the idea that there was any great meaning in what the Beatles were doing. It's his way of saying, "You've got it all wrong, kids. You're looking for profundity and meaning where there is none." A bit harsh, but it was his way of dealing with the fawning adulation, and the Beatles' every gesture being hyper-analyzed.

JD: Lennon for the rest of his life would reject anything thought to be an all-encompassing philosophy—any set code to live your life, whether it was Chairman Mao's "Little Red Book" or Timothy Leary's psychedelic preaching. Yet the things the Beatles learned about the use of sonics in the studio continued to influence a lot of what they did. "Hey Bulldog" is a phenomenal

"Magical Mystery Tour" was about getting on the bus, in the Ken Kesey and the Merry Pranksters sense. The Beatles perform "I Am the Walrus" during the filming of *The Magical Mystery Tour* in September 1967.

Though Lennon especially would reject any overarching philosophies post-*Pepper's*, like the Stones, the Beatles retained elements of the psychedelic.

psychedelic rock song, with some of the most incredible guitar the Beatles ever gave us. "Magical Mystery Tour" is about getting on the bus with Ken Kesey and the Merry Pranksters. "Baby, You're a Rich Man" led to the first big English underground happening, the 14 Hour Technicolour Dream, a phenomenal gathering of these great bands like Tomorrow and Pink Floyd that were inspired by *Revolver* to create some of the most exciting British psychedelic rock. Harrison with "Blue Jay Way" and Lennon with "Across the Universe" and "Glass Onion" and "Dear Prudence"—the sonic influence of psychedelia still can be heard right through to the end of the Beatles' career, even in the midst of an alleged back-to-basics move like the White Album.

GK: Don't forget that double-A-side 1967 single with "Strawberry Fields Forever" and "Penny Lane." I interviewed George Martin years ago, and he said that one of the biggest mistakes he made in overseeing the Beatles' productions was not insisting that those two songs end up on *Sgt. Pepper's*.

JD: It would have made it a better record, but *Revolver* still would have been the stronger effort because they made the same mistake there by not having "Rain" and "Paperback Writer" on the album, which was the original plan.

GK: Right, and yet there are no weak tracks on *Revolver*. *Sgt. Pepper's* has some amazing peaks but a bunch of valleys as well. I look back on *Sgt. Pepper's* and *Satanic Majesties* as period pieces more than anything else. There is some brilliant stuff on both records, but *Sgt. Pepper's* is generally way overrated now, and *Satanic Majesties* is mostly underappreciated. The reality is, they both fall somewhere in the middle in both of these bands' catalogs.

The Maharishi Mahesh Yogi gives an audience to the Beatles and friends in September 1967. Eastern philosophy profoundly affected Harrison for the rest of his life and enabled him to get through the Beatles with a level of dignity.

JD: There is one other aspect we should talk about before we leave the psychedelic years, and that is Brian Jones embracing the sounds of Africa and going to Morocco and Joujouka, and Harrison embracing Indian music.

GK: Those two have a lot in common. Harrison had to fight for every song he got on a record because Lennon and McCartney were so dominant. In the same way, Jagger and Richards were able to edge out Jones. But Jones and Harrison brought in textures and ideas that expanded what the Stones and Beatles were.

JD: I have never been a fan of "Within You Without You" from *Sgt. Pepper's*. I think Harrison did it better on *Revolver* with "Love You To." It's kind of overrated and pretentious, his incorporation of the Indian thing; it can seem insincere. Rather than trying to do what Jones did,

bring these rhythms and instrumental textures into the music at the band's roots, it can sound like Harrison is a jet-setting, culture-appropriating musical dabbler.

GK: I don't agree. Harrison carried on a lot of those ideas throughout his life and career. Once he began playing Eastern music and studying Eastern philosophy, it had a profound effect on the rest of his life and enabled him to get through the Beatles with a level of dignity and self-confidence that he was quickly losing with the way McCartney and Lennon were treating him. With Jones, his transformation from this hardcore blues aficionado is remarkable. He picked up instruments along the way and made them part of the Stones sound. Many of the standout songs from the Stones' psychedelic era bear Jones' imprint because he was willing to go outside the "Chicago rhythm and blues" template he set for the band.

Jones, Richards, and Jagger in Morocco, March 15, 1967.

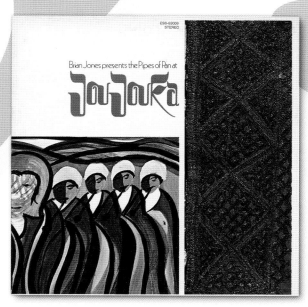

Japanese pressing of Jones' *Pipes of Pan at Joujouka*. Better than Ravi Shankar at *Concert for Bangladesh*?

JD: I'm just saying that as far as the ventures around the globe go, I would rather listen to the 1971 album *Brian Jones Presents: The Pipes of Pan at Joujouka* than again sit through that part of the 1971 *Concert for Bangladesh* where Harrison gives us endless Ravi Shankar.

GK: Yeah, but what about Harrison's terrific 1970 solo album, *All Things Must Pass*? That justifies the trip to the Maharishi right there. A lot of his best Eastern-influenced work came after he was in the Beatles. It was something he could own outside of the Lennon and McCartney monopoly on the Beatles' songwriting.

JD: Well, that I respect, and I really do love George. I just don't want to hear some of his Indian stuff ever again!

BRIAN JONES

THE STONES' ONE-MAN ORCHESTRA

by Greg Kot

Known more for the way he died in 1969 (at twenty-seven in a swimming pool under mysterious circumstances) than his musical accomplishments, Brian Jones is the most unsung of the unsung Stones (basically, everyone who's not named Jagger or Richards). With Keith Richards, Jones developed a give-and-take guitar dialogue that blurred the lines between rhythm and lead playing. Richards may have been King Riff, but it was Jones who played the indelible guitar hook that defined the 1964 hit "The Last Time." Subsequently, Jones developed an uncanny fluidity on just about any instrument he picked up, and the Stones built a string of signature songs around his versatility. Here is a brief look at some of Jones' instrumental contributions. Without them, these Stones classics wouldn't be classics.

"LITTLE RED ROOSTER" *(1964)*
Recorded at Chess Records in Chicago, the Willie Dixon blues standard holds up thanks to Jones' wicked slide guitar.

"PAINT IT, BLACK" *(1965)*
The opening sitar riff conjures a foreboding mood.

"UNDER MY THUMB" *(1966)*
Marimba creates a percussive hook.

"LADY JANE" *(1966)*
Along with Jack Nitzsche's harpsichord, Jones' dulcimer sets the Elizabethan atmosphere.

"GOIN' HOME" *(1966)*
Though Jagger played his share of blues harp on Stones records, Jones played it with Chicago-style flair on many tracks, including this one.

"RUBY TUESDAY" *(1967)*
Jones' oboe melody makes the tune one of the loveliest in the Stones' canon.

"BACKSTREET GIRL" *(1967)*
Jones does double duty on recorder and accordion.

"SHE'S A RAINBOW" *(1967)*
One of the Stones' most ambitious and heavily orchestrated tracks, with Jones at the center of it all, rocking the Mellotron.

"LET'S SPEND THE NIGHT TOGETHER" *(1967)*
Jones' Hammond organ adds weight to this bedroom romp.

"YOU GOT THE SILVER" *(1969)*
In one of Jones' final recording sessions with the band, he picks up an autoharp to accent the country plaintiveness of Keith's vocal.

4

YEAH, I'M THE AXMAN

With the Stones, it's always been about Keef, though Richards never bought into the guitar-hero trip.

JD: Next up in our series of cage matches pitting band members against band members: the guitarists. That means we're talking about George Harrison and John Lennon versus Keith Richards and . . . Brian Jones? Mick Taylor? Ron Wood?

GK: With the Stones, obviously it revolves around Keith, but with him, it was about the band's sound rather than *his* sound. When Brian Jones was in the band, but most of all with Ronnie Wood in the band, you have what Keith has referred to as the "ancient art of weaving"—the blending of the rhythm and the lead guitar duties, to the point where it's pretty hard to tell which is which. It's a very forward-looking approach. In other two-guitar lineups from the Sixties and Seventies, there was a clear dichotomy between the guy on rhythm and the guy on lead, with the lead guy as the star.

This was the era of the guitar hero, remember. But Keith never really thought of the instrument in those terms. His approach was based more on what was going on in Muddy Waters' classic Chicago blues quintet of the early Fifties, with Muddy and Jimmy Rogers on guitars, and the way Jimmy Reed and Eddie Taylor played together on those classic Reed tracks from the Fifties. The roles became only slightly more defined when Mick Taylor was in the band. He was a true virtuoso, and Keith made it a more traditional "you're the lead guitar guy and I'll play everything else" situation at times. I mean, there were things that Taylor could do with the guitar that warranted that sort of showcasing. But even Taylor has said there was a lot of switching off in the roles, so Keith's basic philosophy of having no guitar hierarchy has held sway in the Stones for forty-plus years.

Richards "oiling the machinery" with a Fender Telecaster, the model with which he would become most associated over the years. The band is launching its 1975 Tour of the Americas—incidentally, Ronnie Wood's first with the band—aboard a flatbed truck in New York City.

Above and opposite: Richards and Jones practice "the ancient art of weaving"—the blending of lead and rhythm duties until it's difficult to tell which is which.

JD: Richards has said that when the Stones were forging what would become their signature sound, the idea of "guitar weaving" came from him and Jones sitting and listening to Jimmy Reed albums and really studying them to see how they worked. Keith also has said that his role in the band is "oiling the machinery," though he's really selling himself short. Bill Wyman always maintained that, "Onstage you have to follow Keith. You have no way of *not* following him." And I do think he gets short shrift as an innovator and bandleader. My critical hero, Lester Bangs, who loved bebop and avant-garde jazz as much as he loved raw garage rock, thought that when Keith was playing riffs, he was approaching the guitar the way a great jazz player like John Coltrane would approach a sax solo.

Keith also experimented with other tunings, notably the open G, which, depending on which source you favor, was due to the influence of Ry Cooder, who helped with the solo on "Sister Morphine," or Don Everly, who'd made that a staple of recordings with the Everly Brothers. Wherever it came from, Keith liked it so much that he often removed the low E string from his Telecasters to make it even easier to play in the open G. You can hear that on "Honky Tonk Women" and "Brown Sugar." And it must be said that he loved acoustic guitar as much as electric. Another guitarist might have stayed with an electric ax for songs such as "Brown Sugar," "Jumpin' Jack Flash," or "Street Fighting Man," but Keith makes those tunes by using the acoustic and adding a whole different texture—even if he's distorting the sound on those last two.

GK: Keith is sometimes pigeonholed as the riff guy, and with good reason. But there's more to his game than that. He's a very underrated soloist. He doesn't play a lot of solos, but I'd rate the one he plays on "Sympathy for the Devil" as one of the greatest rock solos of all time. He makes it feel almost tossed off, yet there's a buildup to the crescendo that suggests a great, logical mind at work, the way he uses the space between notes to develop drama. He's a master of economy and, above all, swing. His spiritual mentor was Chuck Berry, and

Berry took that blend of blues and country and imbued it with a jazz player's feel for rhythm. It wasn't just a four-on-the-floor beat—Chuck could make you dance. Keith studied those records and applied that sense of space and movement to his own band. Keith would've fit in very well with someone like Count Basie. And, as you said, even with Charlie Watts and Bill Wyman in the rhythm section, they were following Keith instead of the other way around.

Lennon at the Cavern Club in Liverpool, 1961, with the Rickenbacker 325 he purchased in Hamburg.

Harrison at the Cavern Club, holding a Gretsch and perched on a Vox amp, two quintessential pieces of Beatles gear.

Jones at a recording session, circa 1963.

Richards on the set of *Ready Steady Go!*, June 1964.

Multi-instrumentalist Jones was the roughest and rawest of Richards' six-string partners.
Here he performs with his Vox Phantom Mark III prototype at Empire Pool, London, April 1965.

JD: Shifting to Keith's three six-string wingmen—Jones, Taylor, and Wood—two things they all have in common as guitarists are that they had to adapt to Richards' weaving concept and that they all came forward to add slide guitar at different times. That seems to be a sound Keith loves but one that he never really mastered himself.

Jones was the roughest and rawest of Keith's partners, if you judge him strictly as a guitarist—though he added a whole lot to the band on other instruments (see page 82). But you can't write Brian off completely on guitar because that is where the weaving thing originated.

Next comes a much flashier player, and one with an impressive pedigree. Hertfordshire-raised Michael Kevin "Mick" Taylor had joined John Mayall's Blues Breakers at age seventeen, filling the slot previously held by giants Eric Clapton and Peter Green of Fleetwood Mac. At twenty, he already had a rep as an impressive soloist, but he had to step back a bit to fit in with the Stones and he played a lot of rhythm guitar in tradeoffs with Keith.

GK: Taylor was in many ways a poor fit for the Stones. He didn't really gel with the outlaw personality—he was

It's not a coincidence that many, if not most, Stones fans favor the period from 1969 to 1974, when Mick Taylor served as Richards' foil.

No. 3 (and still Richards' wingman), former Faces guitarist Ronnie Wood replaced Mick Taylor in 1974.

the shy new kid in town, blushing at the Bacchanal. He was also a technically accomplished musician in a band that has never had anyone else of his instrumental caliber, before or since. He played brilliantly in the Stones, adding a melodic flair and a virtuosity that no one could touch. He covered a lot of ground: the Latin vibe he brings to "Can't You Hear Me Knocking," the melancholy beauty of his slide playing on "Moonlight Mile," the climbing, jazz-like solo on "Time Waits for

No One." It's not a coincidence that for a lot of people their favorite version of the Stones was 1969–1974, when Taylor was Richards' foil. But it wasn't meant to last; Taylor really wanted to play jazz and blues, and he felt the Stones weren't giving him a fair shake as a songwriter. So he quit in 1974, just as the Stones were about to record their *Black and Blue* album, and he was soon replaced by Ronnie Wood.

Richards on the set of *Thank Your Lucky Stars*, playing a sunburst Gibson Les Paul outfitted with a Bigsby vibrato tailpiece.

Coke and sympathy. Richards backstage in Lexington, Kentucky, with one of the group's Epiphone guitars and a bottle of Coca-Cola.

Jones tunes up backstage in New York City, 1965.

Jones and friend, Steel Pier, Atlantic City, New Jersey, July 1966. He's playing a Gibson Firebird, which the guitar maker had switched to a non-reverse body style the year before.

Harrison cleans one of his Gretsches during a break in 1963.

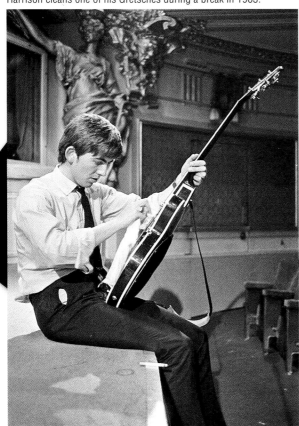

Lennon holds Harrison's Rickenbacker 360/12 on the set of *A Hard Day's Night*, Scala Theatre, London, March 1964.

Lennon and Harrison's Epiphone Casinos flank McCartney's Rickenbacker bass backstage before a concert at the Ernst Merck Halle, Hamburg, June 26, 1966. Lennon later stripped his Casino of its sunburst finish, eventually having it refinished in the natural blonde that was seen in his later years with the Beatles and throughout his solo career.

Harrison displays a pair of Gretsch 6122 Country Gentlemen, 1963.

Wood and Richards—as if they're making it up as they go along.

JD: It may sound a little harsh, but I honestly have never been too impressed with Ronnie's playing in the Stones; to me, it's always seemed as if his primary role in the band has been to shoot pool and do shots with Keith! He isn't the originator that Jones was, or the virtuoso that Taylor was—though, to be fair, Rolling Stones, Inc., didn't want either of those things anymore by the time Wood was tapped to fill out the lineup for those lucrative world tours every few years. They just needed someone to amuse Keith, trade licks with him, and look like he was having a blast while playing "Jumpin' Jack Flash" in a stadium for the ten thousandth time.

GK: Ronnie Wood was no towering, Mick Taylor–style virtuoso, I'll give you that. He was more of a Brian Jones–like utility man, with his ability to play not only guitar but pedal steel, lap steel, slide guitar, and even a little bass—that's his funky bass line on "Emotional Rescue," for example. They didn't just pluck this guy from obscurity. Let's not forget he was already an accomplished songwriter and a key member of one of the U.K.'s best bands, the Faces, when the Stones grabbed him after Taylor walked out. Wood was always about fills and texture, darting in and out of the gaps, and knowing when to sit back to let Keith steer. He

valued songwriting, and like Keith he strongly believed that the instrumentalist's role was to serve the songs, even if that meant playing as few notes as possible. I've seen the Stones two dozen times, and the interplay between Wood and Richards is cool to watch unfolding on stage; there is a casual feel to all of it, like they're reading each others' minds, making it up as they go along, just an extension of their hotel-room jam sessions. Once in a while they'll play lines that unintentionally clash, but then they'll sort of wink at each other from beneath the clouds of cigarette smoke and work themselves out of it as if to say, "Planned that all along." Plus, all that stuff about Wood being Richards' pal shouldn't be underestimated. That Ronnie is relatively low maintenance has a lot to do with the Stones hanging in there for all these years—though some would argue that isn't a good thing!

A more instantly recognizable guitar sound than that of the Stones.

JD: Back to the Beatles, one thing you have to admit about Harrison and Lennon as guitarists is that their sound is a lot more instantly recognizable. Because of Keith's interwoven teamwork thing, you really need Jagger plus Richards to evoke the Stones' sound, whereas all you need is five or six notes of an introductory riff from Harrison to get "Beatles!" Think of "Day Tripper" and the sound of George's guitar, or the chiming quality of that Rickenbacker in "A Hard

Day's Night" or "Help!"—it just goes on forever. Along with the stacked vocal harmonies, *that* is the sound of the Beatles.

GK: Yes, though innocent bystanders often overlook George's contributions because he was so self-effacing, so averse to calling attention to himself. George played exactly what the song needed, nothing more, nothing less. He defined "A Hard Day's Night" with just one

Harrison in 1964 with his Rickenbacker 360/12, the twelve-string that famously kicks off "A Hard Day's Night."

One brilliant chord, right at the start. Big in Japan, too.

brilliant chord, right at the start. How many guitarists can say that?

JD: George is the Beatles' lead guitarist, but as distinctive as his sound is, he's not flashy. Like Keith, he's a team player—echoing melody lines, adding counterpoint, or inserting a riff to provide the hook exactly where it's needed. Andy Babiuk, who wrote the book *Beatles Gear: All the Fab Four's Instruments, from Stage to Studio*, said, "That was his gift. It's hard to imagine those songs without the bits George came up with. Divorce any one of them from the track, and the song just doesn't sound right." As for Lennon's guitar-playing, he knew to stay in the background and just add whatever was needed. He wasn't the most technically gifted guitar player, but he knew his role as a rhythm guitarist.

GK: He was a great rhythm guitar player, albeit with a different approach than Keith's. If you listen to the

Beatles' live sets in Hamburg, that's the sound of Lennon driving the band. He was relentless. When the Beatles rocked hardest, it was usually John pushing the tempo.

JD: Ultimately, it's tough to call a winner in this one, and it comes down to personal preference and what you really value in a guitar player: Solos or riffs, teamwork or stealing the spotlight?

GK: Keith and George especially would be appalled that someone would single them out as these extraordinary guitar players who stood above the bands. What they valued most was their ability to complement the band.

JD: What would you rather have? A gourmet French meal cooked by a three-star chef or the ideal dinner cooked by an Italian grandmother? I'd have them both, at opposite ends of the same week! They're such different and equally innovative and influential guitarists, I think we just have to call this one a tie.

KEITH RICHARDS

THE BEST OF THE HUMAN RIFF

by Greg Kot

One of rock's great rhythm guitarists, Keith Richards is, above all, the master of the riff, the instrumental refrains that launched dozens of Stones songs. Here are a handful of his best.

"(I CAN'T GET NO) SATISFACTION" *(1965)*
Fuzz-tone sustain defines the three-note nod to Martha and the Vandellas' "Dancing in the Street."

"JUMPIN' JACK FLASH" *(1968)*
Keith plays an acoustic guitar through an overloaded cassette-player microphone and launches the Stones' greatest era.

"STREET FIGHTING MAN" *(1968)*
The same methodology behind "Jumpin' Jack Flash," this time with multiple acoustic guitars.

"GIMME SHELTER" *(1969)*
A tremolo effect through deteriorating amplifiers soaks the song in dread; the gigantic riff was concocted on a borrowed acoustic guitar, which promptly broke after the first take.

"BITCH" *(1971)*
A guitar line so relentless, the horns jump all over it and wrestle it for supremacy.

"CAN'T YOU HEAR ME KNOCKING" *(1971)*
There's the open-tuned riff that opens the door, and then there's the lengthy guitar jam that blows through it.

"TUMBLING DICE" *(1972)*
At times all the other instruments drop away to allow the unhurried but absolutely splendid riff to tumble down like a pair of sevens.

"HAND OF FATE" *(1975)*
Keith sets a hard-edged tone while guest guitarist Al Perkins weaves around it.

"BEAST OF BURDEN" *(1978)*
This soul ballad just rolls out after Keith sets the mood with a beautifully lyrical intro and then jabs in and out with Ronnie Wood.

"START ME UP" *(1981)*
It started out as a reggae song, until Keith's guitar transformed it.

GEORGE HARRISON

WHILE HIS GUITAR GENTLY WEEPS

by Greg Kot

George Harrison is rarely mentioned when "rock's greatest guitarists" are discussed. He wasn't as flamboyant as Jimi Hendrix or Jeff Beck. He didn't have the same tortured obsession with the blues and Robert Johnson as his pal Eric Clapton. He didn't exude the auteur-like charisma of a Jimmy Page. But Harrison endures because he epitomized concision, restraint, and unerring taste. And it's no wonder: He was a disciple of Carl Perkins and Scotty Moore, guitarists who embroidered the melody and served the songs rather than their egos. Here are George's finest moments as a Beatles guitarist.

"I SAW HER STANDING THERE" *(1964)*
A reverb-drenched solo that Scotty Moore would've been proud to plug into one of Elvis Presley's sessions at Sun Studios in Memphis.

"EVERYBODY'S TRYING TO BE MY BABY" *(1964)*
Harrison pays tribute to his hero Carl Perkins with some ferocious be-bop-baby picking on the *Live at the BBC* album.

"A HARD DAY'S NIGHT" *(1965)*
The chord heard 'round the world (from the school of Glenn Miller jazz harmonics) opens the song and closes it (in arpeggio).

"NORWEGIAN WOOD" *(1965)*
The self-taught sitar player introduces Indian drone to the Beatles lexicon.

"IF I NEEDED SOMEONE" *(1965)*
Roger McGuinn says he picked up a twelve-string Rickenbacker after he saw Harrison play one in *A Hard Day's Night*. Here, Harrison returns the favor with a folk-rock jangler that bows toward McGuinn and the Byrds' "The Bells of Rhymney."

"TAXMAN" *(1966)*
Tough-as-nails rhythm guitar (later appropriated by the Jam) matches the spite and sarcasm in Harrison's lyrics.

"I'M ONLY SLEEPING" *(1966)*
With psychedelic rock ascendant, Harrison provides a defining moment with his backward guitar solo.

"WITHIN YOU WITHOUT YOU" *(1967)*
Amid this dreamy excursion down the raga-rock rabbit hole, Harrison's sitar dances with a string section.

"WHILE MY GUITAR GENTLY WEEPS" *(1968)*
Eric Clapton plays the famous solo on the White Album version, but Harrison's acoustic take on *Anthology 3* is luminous and haunting, presaging the entire career of Elliot Smith.

"HERE COMES THE SUN" *(1969)*
The guitar intro is a song in itself.

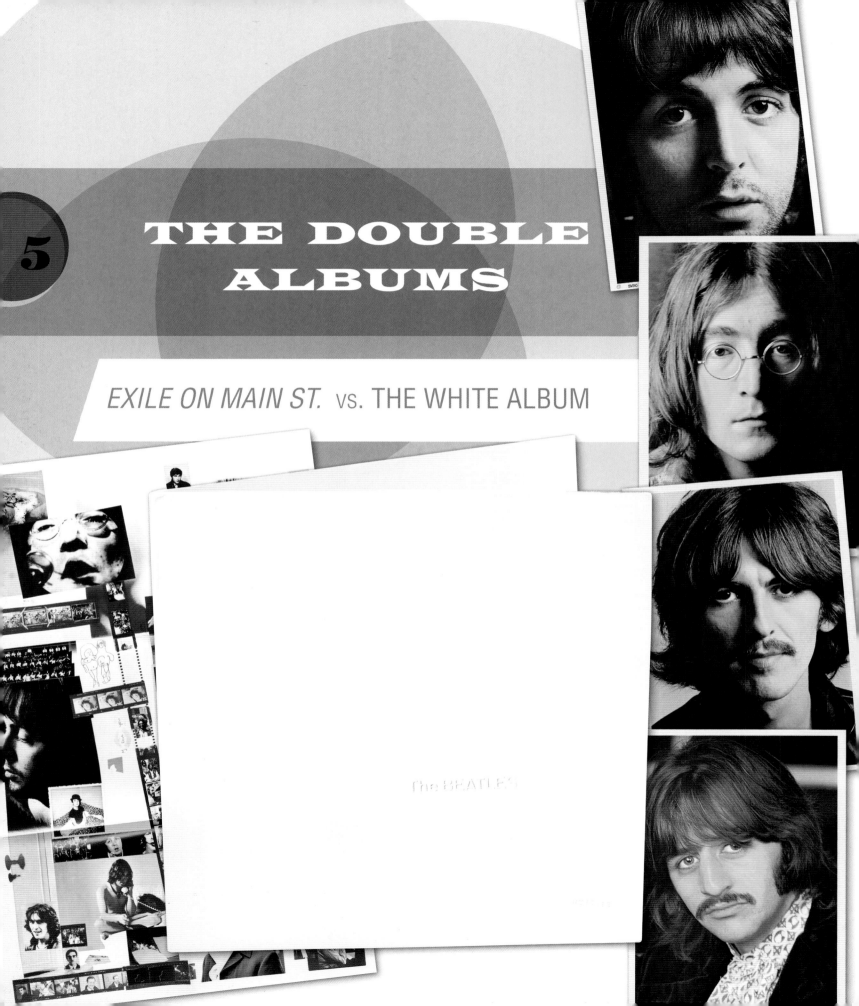

5

THE DOUBLE ALBUMS

EXILE ON MAIN ST. vs. THE WHITE ALBUM

Jagger weds Bianca Pérez Moreno de Macías in St. Tropez, France, May 12, 1971, just prior to the start of the *Exile* sessions, as Richards, Pallenberg, and their son, Marlon, look on. Tension between the two women affected the already dark vibe at Richards' nearby rented mansion, where the double album was being made.

JD: Since both of these bands issued double albums, it makes sense for us to take a look at *Exile on Main St.* and *The Beatles*, better known, of course, as the White Album, and compare them as epic statements. Still, aside from the gatefold sleeves and the more-generous-than-usual bounty of music that each of these sets contains, these are fundamentally different records, don't you think?

GK: They are fundamentally different records—the White Album recorded and released in 1968, and *Exile on Main St.* issued in 1972—but the bands were in similar places in their careers. They were iconic bands at a very fragile time, in the process of falling apart rather than exhibiting the all-for-one spirit that characterized the early phases of their careers. The White Album was basically the Beatles working in three studios, often separately. John Lennon described the sessions as solo tracks backed by the other guys. As for *Exile*, Jagger

was in and out of the sessions. The band was more like a guerilla outfit, meeting at night with different people showing up each time.

One of the interesting issues was the rivalry that was developing between the Rolling Stones' wives at the time. Mick had just married Bianca Pérez Morena de Macías, and Keith's significant other, Anita Pallenberg, was not a big fan of Bianca. The band was recording in Keith's mansion in the south of France, and Bianca was basically persona non grata because Anita didn't want her there. Mick felt bad about that—"If she's not welcome here, then I won't be hanging around"—so he wasn't the full-time presence that he had been on earlier Stones albums.

JD: Right. It's famously said that *Their Satanic Majesties Request* was an album made under the influence of bail, but we all know that *Exile on Main St.* was an album made under the influence of heroin, along with

Lennon and McCartney hold a press conference in New York City on May 14, 1968, to announce the launch of Apple.

just about any other substance that can be ingested or abused, as well as jealousy, sexual intrigue, and plain old bad blood. Various other Stones were missing in action for different parts of the recordings too, and some great session players filled in. The instruments were set up in the basement of Keith's chateau, and these guys were getting together, getting wasted, and making music. Yet despite that messy scenario, *Exile* remains the most unified album in the Stones' catalog in terms of creating a strange but consistent vibe from beginning to end, and that's where the huge difference with the White Album comes in because *The Beatles*, stylistically, is all over the map.

But, you're right in that both bands were at each others' throats, and they were sick and tired of celebrity and the downsides of fame, even as they were enjoying the privileges of it. These musicians all were wondering what it was all about at this point in their careers, and they were trying to get back to what they loved about making music in the first place.

One of the Beatles' rare recorded collaborations in the summer of 1968—lending their voices to *Yellow Submarine*.

GK: It's amazing how well both of these albums came out, given the working conditions. Jagger has been quoted numerous times saying that he hated the sessions for *Exile*, and the vibe wasn't good. They were recording in this dank basement, it was really humid, the instruments were consistently going out of tune, and the work days were basically, "We play until Keith passes out." Sometimes the sessions would last three or four days because Keith was like a vampire who never emerged from his lair lest he see the sunlight. He'd get on one of his benders and work on music for days, and whoever could hang with him got to play on the song. There were some tracks where producer Jimmy Miller was on drums because Charlie wasn't available when Keith was itching to cut a track at 3 a.m. after being up for seventy-two hours. On "Happy," you have Miller on drums, saxophonist Bobby Keys playing a little percussion, and Keith playing everything else.

Ditto for the White Album. A number of tracks had just one Beatle playing by himself, or the others only peripherally involved. But in terms of the strength of the albums, *Exile* is thought of as the Stones' definitive album, and many people call it the greatest rock album of all time. Do you think the Beatles' White Album belongs in the same category? Is it the same kind of definitive statement for the Beatles that many people consider *Exile* to be for the Stones?

JD: Absolutely not. The White Album to me is very much a collection of songs. Some of them absolutely play to the Beatles' strengths, and some of them underscore their weaknesses. I think the last album the Beatles made that was very much of a piece was *Sgt. Pepper's Lonely Hearts Club Band*, which we've already argued about. The White Album, on the other hand, is a bunch of songs with just the words *The*

McCartney walks alone on the grounds of his father's home in July 1968.

Beatles on a stark white cover—a blank slate—as if to say, "We're a lot of different things, and here is a collection of the whole mess of what we are." *Exile* is more cohesive, even if that nonsensical cover collage hints at the opposite. You just can't get around the unity of the sound developed in that putrid basement, or the thematic concerns that run through the whole album. It's a record about the search for redemption while you're in the midst of a deep depression, the search for a glimmer of light from the bottom of a deep, dark well. It's the Stones at their best, starting with the blues but taking it somewhere entirely new.

The Stones had seen the Sixties' utopian dream of peace and love and community proven false at Altamont—not that they ever really bought into all that hippie hoo-ha. You add to that the nonstop swirl of fame and celebrity and overindulgence, and you have a group of musicians in a very dark place, struggling to get out.

The Beatles are in a place of artistic frustration, and yet they still remain—with the exception of Lennon, when he's flashing his mean and cynical streaks—a relatively sunny pop band. I mean, there is no "Rocky Racoon" on *Exile on Main St.*!

As Keith Moerer wrote in a book I edited called *Kill Your Idols*, it's hard to talk about *Exile* and not sound as if you're glorifying the druggie decadence of the record. A lot of people would not survive the kind of abuse that the Rolling Stones had put themselves through, and it's one of the most destructive lies in rock history that you have to live that life of excess in order to make great art. So one thing I want to make clear is that, in lauding the sound and the vibe and the themes of a search for redemption on this record, I'm not championing the way the band was living in order to get there, and it really is a miracle that most of the group is still alive!

Harrison disembarks a flight from India with sitar in hand, followed by wife Pattie Boyd and Starr, June 1968.

GK: One of the reasons *Exile* is so celebrated is that the songs complement one another. It's an album in the classic sense of that word. If you're just looking at individual moments and going song for song, the Beatles might have a stronger set of pop tunes—songs that can be pulled off the album and played as singles that a broad audience can relate to without the context of the album. Whereas, if you pull tracks off *Exile*, they sound orphaned. I'm thinking of some of the less celebrated tracks, which are more about vibe than songcraft: "Casino Boogie" . . .

JD: . . . "Ventilator Blues" . . .

GK: . . . "Just Wanna See His Face." All vibe! These moments embody the murk of *Exile*, the decay, the

sound of instruments and emotions breaking down, the sessions going for days at a time where time almost seems to stand still, and there is no sense of whether it is day or night or why it even matters. So the songs became snapshots of a bender in progress, like you're eavesdropping on these guys losing their minds together over a period of time in this isolated, dark place. The Beatles' record does not have that cohesiveness. It definitely has more of a hodgepodge element to it, more of a sense of "Here are a bunch of songs and we're competing with one another and we're each trying to outdo one another, but we're not necessarily collaborating with one another." It's no longer about the whole being greater than the sum of its parts. The White Album is the first hint that the Beatles aren't really functioning as a band anymore but as a collection of solo artists in waiting.

Richards, wife Anita Pallenberg, and their son, Marlon, at Villa Nellcôte, May 1971.

Take Lennon's "Yer Blues." Whereas the Stones are saturated in the blues, the Beatles have barely any trace of it in much of their music. Then Lennon does this near-parody of it. It's like, "You want the deepest, darkest blues ever? The loneliest, saddest, most suicidal blues? I'm going to give it to you." It's a template for the Plastic Ono Band record. It has that same sense of despair and purging. I don't think it's the kind of song that the Beatles, when they were really collaborating, ever would have put on a Beatles album.

JD: Even at their darkest, the Beatles are never as scary as the Stones, though. The Fabs did try to inject a little horror into the White Album—no surprise, since the storm clouds were everywhere in '68—and obviously, "Helter Skelter" has acquired a spooky afterlife, since it was adopted by the Manson Family. If you put that out of your mind, it's a frantic song but nowhere near Stones-scary. Same with "Everybody's Got Something to Hide Except Me and My Monkey," which is really frenetic, but not a Stones-level, speed-driven freak-out. To me, "Happiness Is a Warm Gun" is the most frightening tune the Beatles ever recorded—not really on the face of it, but in the juxtaposition of an advertising-jingle-worthy melody and chorus with a very dark celebration of violence and its primary instrument.

Again, though, I don't want to overdramatize the Stones as Satanic Majesties and say they really were bigger badasses than the Hells Angels or whatever other villains you care to name. A lot of that is skillful self-mythologizing in the best tradition of the blues, à la Robert Johnson selling his soul at the crossroads. I mean, Richards apparently liked to brag that the Villa Nellcôte, that mansion he was renting in France, had been the Gestapo headquarters in the area, but I don't think he really was or wanted to be a Nazi. It was useful marketing—an extension of what they'd been doing since the beginning.

Going back to that white cover of *The Beatles*: It seems to me that the group is trying to strip all of the poses away and not market themselves as anything at all on their ninth album. Meanwhile, the Stones are almost doing a concept album with *Exile*, their tenth record.

GK: To me, the White Album's cover conveys one message loud and clear: "This is a back-to-basics record." It's the Beatles' version of a roots record, in contrast to the studio-as-instrument experimentation that had been their preferred method of working since *Rubber Soul*. The acoustic demos for the White Album set the tone, and they are extraordinary. Harrison's acoustic version of "While My Guitar Gently Weeps" is as good as the full-band version with Eric Clapton on guitar.

In a lot of ways, you feel sorry for Harrison because he was consistently the third wheel. He was the songwriter whose songs didn't quite measure up to the hallowed duo of McCartney and Lennon. He had to fight for everything, and the only way he felt they were going to take him seriously with "While My Guitar Gently Weeps" was if he pulled in Clapton to play on it. "With Eric here, they can't possibly reject it or make fun of me."

This came up consistently in the recording sessions with the latter-day Beatles. When a guest showed up, the Beatles were on their best behavior, trying to get along and refocusing on the music. It worked for the Stones, too. On *Exile*, the ancillary players have crucial roles. My favorite track on *Exile* has always been "Let It Loose." It's a ballad, by far the longest song on the record, and it has this New Orleans soul vibe because Dr. John basically brought in a bunch of his friends to sing backing vocals on it. That was one of the few tracks that wasn't recorded in France; it was actually cut in Los Angeles. But the vibe fits, and it's because of these outside players—these deeply American musicians and singers—being a part of it. The Stones were such huge fans of American music—gospel, blues, New Orleans R&B—and they filter their druggy rock-star trip through those idioms on *Exile*. Bobby Keys' saxophone—the Stones loved that Texas grit. Billy Preston's funk-gospel organ on "Shine a Light." The boogie blues of Slim Harpo on "Hip Shake." *Exile* is the Stones' ultimate homage to American music.

Deeply American influences such as Slim Harpo (upper left) and guest musicians like Dr. John (upper right), Billy Preston (lower left), and Bobby Keys (lower right) permeated *Exile* and helped the Stones create their ultimate homage to American music.

JD: I think they finally perfected what they'd been trying to do all along. They were no longer white upper-middle-class Englishmen trying to play their version of black American blues—they'd finally transformed those influences into a blues all their own. When they cover Slim Harpo's "Hip Shake" and Robert Johnson's "Stop Breaking Down," those songs aren't even recognizable anymore as great American blues tunes. They've become something else—Rolling Stones music, pure and simple. More than any other album in their catalog, *Exile* defines that.

For me, two more defining moments on the record are "Rocks Off" and "Shine a Light." "Rocks Off" sets the tone for the entire album with that incredible opium/psychedelic breakdown in the middle of the song and the refrain, *"I can only get my rocks off when*

I'm dreaming." Having experienced every decadent pleasure that life can offer, these musicians have nowhere to go anymore except to fantasize—or to look to the heavens. That's where "Shine a Light" comes in. The effect of *Exile* as a whole is like a bad trip on psychedelics, but as awful as the trip is, there's a moment of crystalline clarity that comes with the dawn. There is no such journey on the Beatles' album.

You mentioned the competition among the songwriters. Except for the Indian excursions, Harrison consistently came forward with really good songs on all of the Beatles' albums. "While My Guitar Gently Weeps" obviously is a classic, but even "Piggies" is a great tune—a lot of bands would have killed to have one song that strong, but with the Beatles, it's just another George song tossed into the middle of the White Album. On the

Before they fled the U.K.'s burdensome taxes, the Stones did a tour of the U.K. Richards and Wyman at the Roundhouse, London, March 14, 1971.

other hand, I think that with the slots given to Ringo as vocalist here, they're really scraping the bottom of the barrel. "Good Night" is just a dreadful piece of schmaltz, and "Don't Pass Me By" is an instantly forgettable piece of generic rockabilly. And what about some of McCartney's songs? "Rocky Racoon"—really?

GK: Oh, c'mon. "Rocky Racoon" is funny, a talking-blues parody, combined with some cool acoustic finger-picking that he picked up from Donovan on their trip to India to visit the Maharishi. But "Wild Honey Pie" does annoy me. That's McCartney tossing one off, and it's telling that none of the other Beatles play on it. How that got on the album at the expense of a strong Harrison track like "Sour Milk Sea" is puzzling. "The Continuing Story of Bungalow Bill" is a weak track from

Lennon, and "Martha My Dear" is another trifling track from McCartney, written music-hall style about his pet sheepdog. Please!

JD: Or "Mother Nature's Son"—I mean, really, Paul. What are you trying to do? "Let's throw one to the hippies' 'back to earth' movement?"

GK: I love the acoustic picking, though. It's surpassed only by "Blackbird," which is one of McCartney's best songs in that mode. The acoustic finger-picking had a big influence on the amazing demos for the White Album. Talk about a back-to-basics record—in many ways, the Beatles might have been better off releasing the spare acoustic versions of many of these songs.

A billboard on Sunset Strip in Los Angeles announces the release of *Exile on Main St.* and the Stones' West Coast tour dates.

JD: Well, if we're playing fantasy baseball, I would really love to see a movie made à la *Sympathy for the Devil* to show us what those sessions at Nellcôte were really like!

GK: A few X-rated scenes with long stretches of people passed out on the floor.

JD: Still, there is always the possibility that they were really just sitting around drinking tea and eating scones! It's what I was saying about playing to the bad-boy mythology: We really don't know for certain how much of the decadence was real and how much was mythology.

GK: With Gram Parsons skulking around the mansion with Keith, I doubt there was a whole lot of healthy activity going around at that time. But as you said, that's the disturbing mythology of that record. At the same time, there is a redemptive quality in the music; it was one of the things that kept Keith Richards alive. As long as there was music to be made, Keith had a reason to keep going. You do not stay up for days at a time unless you're on a mission of some sort, and Keith was definitely on a mission.

With the Beatles, I sense a certain lack of direction. They don't have anyone in charge like the Stones had Richards. And they're pulling their punches. It's interesting that the version of "Revolution" that came out as a single was a hard rocker, while on the White Album it's slowed down, almost passive. Lennon was dubious about the power of music to effect change. On his own he would write strident songs like "Power to the People" and "Imagine," where he was embracing

the idea that a song actually could change the world. But the atmosphere around the Beatles was so toxic at the time that there was a certain amount of cynicism creeping into all of their songs, especially Lennon's. In "Glass Onion," he mocks the Beatles' fans for their obsessiveness. And on "Happiness Is a Warm Gun," he mocks everything else. It's the album's most representative moment. There is a level of sarcasm that encapsulates Lennon's attitude about everything: politics, marketing, the world, the state of the Beatles. At the same time, it's a brilliant song. It's basically a four-part, mini-history of rock 'n' roll in which he goes through everything from doo-wop to heavy metal in the span of a few minutes.

JD: Here's another fantasy: It would have been fascinating to boil down the White Album to a single disc of all of those darker moments. If you had "Dear Prudence," "Glass Onion," "Happiness Is a Warm Gun," and even "Blackbird"—which, I agree, is McCartney at his best; Mr. Obvious for once waxing metaphorical and singing about African-Americans in very moving terms—what would that single album sound like? I'd also include "Everybody's Got Something to Hide Except Me and My Monkey," "Sexy Sadie," "Helter Skelter," and "Revolution 1," though I, too, prefer the upbeat, nasty single version. Now *that* is a really powerful record, and one that has a vibe, not unlike *Exile*. On the other hand, "Don't Pass Me By," "Why Don't We Do It in the Road?," "I Will," "Julia," and "Wild Honey Pie"—if you put all of those together, that's a record I could live without ever hearing again.

Stevie Wonder joins the Stones onstage at Madison Square Garden, New York City, July 26, 1972. Wonder was the Stones' opening act on their infamous thirty-city tour of the United States and Canada.

GK: Well, I'll make a case for some of those slower songs. Lennon's "Julia" was as personal a song as he had written to that point. Here, again, we're seeing Lennon presaging his solo albums. He's dropping broad hints: "I'm not about this band anymore. I'm getting into this more personal space." The introspection of "Julia" points to an even deeper exploration of the same subject, "Mother," a few years later. I also have to make a case for Harrison with a song like "Long, Long, Long," a hymn-like testament to his faith that anticipates his first solo album, *All Things Must Pass*.

I look at the White Album as a transitional work—the four Beatles laying the groundwork for how they would spend the rest of their lives away from their band mates—while *Exile* is Keith Richards' defining statement as a Rolling Stone. For the rest of the decade, he was pretty much out of it because of his drug and legal troubles, and Mick effectively took over the band.

JD: Aside from both of these albums being about bands pulling apart; and both of them, to a degree, being about the Sixties dream withering and dying, and both, of course, being double albums, what else do they have in common? I really don't want to know anyone who doesn't believe that *Exile on Main St.* is a masterpiece. I sure don't feel that way about the White Album.

GK: I love the White Album, but it's deeply flawed—a fascinating glimpse into the dysfunction of the most famous rock band in the world at the time. The Beatles really weren't all on the same page, and some crappy songs snuck through quality control. *Exile* was also made during a dysfunctional time in the Stones' history, but it had Keith Richards as the sheriff, and he kept the music at a high level. As a full-on rock record, it has few peers: "Rocks Off," "Happy," "Tumbling Dice," and especially "Rip This Joint." The demons come out on that one, like they were inventing punk rock by speeding up Chuck Berry. *Exile* has become the blueprint for how a rock band with two guitars, a bass, drums, and a vocalist should sound, even though sometimes it was an illusion of a band because all the guys weren't there for all the songs. Whereas the White Album is the exact opposite: Here is what a band sounds like when its four members are in every-man-for-himself mode. It's disparate, at times brilliant, but padded with filler.

JD: Maybe that's the key: *Exile* is a rock album in that it's about a vibe and an attitude and a sound from start to finish. *The Beatles* is a pop album in that it's about the songs, and it rises and falls in quality depending on the strength of the particular track you're playing.

FINGERPRINT FILE

THE SCANDALS AND THE TRAGEDIES

by Jim DeRogatis

THE SHOTS HEARD 'ROUND THE WORLD

On December 8, 1980, at about 10:50 p.m., a deranged fan, Mark David Chapman, shot John Lennon four times in the back outside the Dakota apartment building in New York City. Lennon was pronounced dead on arrival at Roosevelt Hospital at 11:07 p.m. Chapman pled guilty to second-degree murder and was sentenced to twenty years to life; he has been eligible for parole since 2000 but has regularly been denied and continues to be held at Attica State Prison.

On December 6, 1969, the Rolling Stones held their ill-advised, quickly organized free concert at the Altamont Speedway, between the towns of Tracy and Livermore in Northern California. There were four deaths: two caused by a hit-and-run driver, one drowning in an irrigation canal, and, infamously, the stabbing of a young black man, Meredith Hunter, by a Hells Angel, Alan Passaro. Hunter had pulled a gun, and Passaro was acquitted by a jury that held that he acted in self-defense.

The Altamont mayhem gets rolling as Stones tour manager Sam Cutler (left) and promoter Michael Lang (right) look on from the stage.

Fans keep vigil outside Lennon's Manhattan apartment, December 11, 1980.

SEX, SEX, AND MORE SEX

Fans often think the Stones had it all over the Beatles when it came to wild Bacchanals (see the Mars Bar story on the next page, for a start, or any book ever written about the band), but no less an authority than Lennon said that the Fabs were just better at keeping their priapic excesses under cover, so to speak. In a 1970 interview with *Rolling Stone*, he compared life in the Beatles to the orgies of ancient Rome, saying, "If you couldn't get groupies, we had whores. Whatever was going. There were photos of me crawling 'round on my knees coming out of whorehouses in Amsterdam with people saying, 'Good morning, John!'"

As for same-sex adventures, there's more smoke than fire. Speculation persists that Lennon slept with Brian Epstein while the two were on holiday, even though the musician sometimes cruelly mocked the manager for being gay—for example, reportedly cracking that Epstein's autobiography, *A Cellarful of Noise*, should have been titled *A Cellarful of Boys*. Meanwhile, plenty of fans still believe that Jagger slept with David Bowie, though both have denied it, and the story seems to have been started as a bid for publicity by Bowie's ex-wife, Angela (who apparently was not, also contrary to the rumors, the inspiration for the Stones' "Angie").

Harrison and Boyd, 1966.

THE LOVE TRIANGLES

For the Stones, it was Brian Jones, Keith Richards, and Anita Pallenberg. Richards won; the couple was together from 1967 to 1979 and had three children.

For the Beatles, it was George Harrison, Pattie Boyd, and Eric Clapton. The Harrison–Boyd marriage ended after eleven years in 1977; Clapton and Boyd were then married from 1979 to 1988. Clapton famously wrote "Layla" in 1970 about his then unrequited love.

Richards with Pallenberg, whom he wooed away from Jones.

THE MOST CELEBRATED BUSTS

Though the Rolling Stones' first bust is, by far, the most entertaining—Mick Jagger, Bill Wyman, and Brian Jones were arrested on March 18, 1965, and charged with public urination after they were turned away from a gas-station toilet in West Ham, England—the most famous happened at Keith Richards' country estate, Redlands, on February 12, 1967, when twenty officers raided the house, found assorted drugs and paraphernalia, and charged Richards and Jagger with possession. Contrary to the legend, however, they did not find Jagger in the act of eating a Mars Bar lodged in a certain orifice of his then girlfriend, Marianne Faithfull. In her autobiography, Faithfull debunked this oft-repeated legend, writing, "The Mars Bar was a very effective piece of demonizing. *Way* out there. . . . It's a dirty old man's fantasy. . . . A cop's idea of what people do on acid!"

Smartly dressed and seemingly nonchalant, Jagger and Richards leave court after an appearance regarding their infamous 1967 drug bust.

Leaving court after answering charges of public urination at a petrol station, July 22, 1965. Watts and Richards were on hand as character witnesses.

As for the Beatles' busts, Lennon and Yoko Ono were arrested at their home in London on October 19, 1968, and charged with drug possession a few days after the couple announced that Ono was pregnant, creating a scandal because both were still married to other people. (The pregnancy ended in a miscarriage shortly after the arrest.) George Harrison was arrested and charged with marijuana possession on March 12, 1969, by the same officer who arrested Lennon and Ono. (The officer later was charged with conspiracy to pervert the course of justice for planting drugs in many of his cases.) But the most notorious Beatles arrest happened long after the group broke up, when Paul McCartney was detained in Japan in 1980 for carrying more than half a pound of marijuana in his luggage. He spent nine days in a Tokyo jail before being deported and lost more than $350,000 when he had to cancel his group Wings' Japanese tour dates.

Harrison, with wife Pattie Boyd, addresses the media after being fined £250 for cannabis possession, March 30, 1969.

Lennon and Ono after a court appearance for their 1968 marijuana bust.

LOOSE LIPS

No contest here: The Beatles easily beat the Stones when it comes to controversial comments, thanks to Lennon's statement to his friend, reporter Maureen Cleave, printed in England's *Evening Standard* on March 4, 1966. "Christianity will go," he told Cleave. "It will vanish and shrink. I needn't argue with that; I'm right and I will be proved right. We're more popular than Jesus now; I don't know which will go first—rock 'n' roll or Christianity. Jesus was alright, but his disciples were thick and ordinary. It's them twisting it that ruins it for me."

Ignored in Britain at the time, the comment was reprinted in the U.S. teen magazine *Datebook* five months later, on July 29. Reduced to "We're more popular than Jesus now," it caused a furor that included record burnings, radio boycotts, death threats, and a protest by the Ku Klux Klan at a Beatles concert in Alabama. Lennon eventually made a tortured apology: "If I had said television is more popular than Jesus, I might have got away with it, but I just happened to be talking to a friend and I used the word 'Beatles' as a remote thing, not as what I think—as Beatles, as those other Beatles like other people see us. I just said 'they' are having more influence on kids and things than anything else, including Jesus. But I said it in that way which is the wrong way."

Teenagers in Jackson, Mississippi, burn records, books, and wigs to protest Lennon's "bigger than Jesus" comment.

THE SILLIEST RUMORS

Keith beat his heroin addiction by having all of his blood drained and replaced in a Swiss medical clinic. "It was a joke," Richards has said. "I was fucking sick of answering that question"—how he'd cleaned up—"so I gave them a story."

Paul is dead. He isn't, at least not as of this writing. On the other hand, if we accept that he died in November 1966 and was replaced by a lookalike and soundalike, that might explain how one of the geniuses who made *Revolver* later came to record "Ebony and Ivory" and "Silly Love Songs."

THE TRAGIC DEATHS BEFORE THEIR TIMES

At around midnight, July 2–3, 1969, Brian Jones was discovered lying on the bottom of the swimming pool at his home at Cotchford Farm, Sussex, a house formerly owned by *Winnie-the-Pooh* author A. A. Milne. By the time the ambulance arrived, he was pronounced dead at age twenty-seven, with the coroner's report declaring "death by misadventure" and noting a liver and heart damaged by drug and alcohol abuse.

On April 10, 1962, the Beatles' friend and former band mate Stu Sutcliffe died of cerebral paralysis; he was twenty-one. And on August 27, 1967, Epstein was found dead of a drug overdose, the result of taking six Carbitrals mixed with alcohol. (He had regularly been taking the sedative and had built up a dangerous tolerance.)

Stu Sutcliffe in Hamburg, 1961.

Beatles fans read of Epstein's death on the steps of his London home.

Cotchford Farm and the swimming pool where Jones met his demise.

6 GET TO THE BOTTOM

THE BASSISTS

Convention Center, Las Vegas, Nevada, August 20, 1964.

JD: Continuing with the instrumentalist matchups, it's bass player against bass player. I love Bill Wyman. He wrote one of my favorite books on the Stones—*Stone Alone*—and I think he was exactly the presence that crazy band needed, just standing in the shadows and holding down the bottom. But no doubt about it, McCartney is the bass ace. He wins hands down.

GK: He is absolutely one of the greatest bass players ever. He redefined how the bass could be played in the Sixties alongside people like James Jamerson of Motown, who was a huge influence, Brian Wilson in the Beach Boys, and, of course, Jack Bruce and John Entwistle, his peers in the English rock scene. McCartney brought an ultra-melodic approach to bass by playing counterpoint lines that are among the most beautiful parts of those Beatles songs. Even on the early Beatles recordings, Paul's bass is mixed fairly high. Wyman's bass is mixed very low, and it's sometimes difficult to pick out his parts in Stones songs. Yet if you pull Bill's parts out, the songs would lose something essential. Both guys had a particular role to play in their bands, and they played it well.

Wyman knew his role as one half of the Stones' "Engine Room."

JD: It could be a function of ego, too. I always thought it was interesting that McCartney played that Hofner bass, which looks more like a guitar than a bass. I think he wanted to be a driving force in the band, whether he was singing one of his own tunes or backing up the other guys on the songs that they wrote. No matter what he was doing, he wanted to be noticed. His way of doing that was to play incredibly melodically. The difference between a Wyman bass part and a McCartney bass part is that you can hum a McCartney part. The melodies are key, and he inserts himself as a melodic force while at the same time holding down the rhythm. He is interacting with both the vocals and the guitars, instead of just the guitars and the drums, and it is unique and very musical. I can't picture him just doing what Wyman did. Wyman, despite knowing the jazz world, really saw his role in the Stones as coming from the blues, and in the blues, the bassist supports the guitarist, plain and simple. So Bill is pounding out the rhythm and the root chords. In the jazz world, you had a lot of virtuoso bassists—there is no Charlie Mingus in Bill Wyman—whereas in the blues world, it's hard to really name one, aside from Willie Dixon. Wyman could do a bit of a Motown thing from time to time, but I think he saw himself in a supporting, background role, while McCartney wanted to grab the spotlight. That's the difference.

Hamburg, 1960, when McCartney was one of the band's three guitarists. Erstwhile member and former bassist Stu Sutcliffe is in the background.

"Look at me!" McCartney approached the bass like a guitarist.

With his ultramelodic approach, McCartney absolutely defined how the bass could be played in a rock 'n' roll band.

With the trademark Hofner "violin bass" on the set of *Thank Your Lucky Stars*, London, July 11, 1964.

Wyman lets down his stoic mask, 1963.

With a Vox Teardrop bass, Stadthalle, Bremen, West Germany, March 29, 1967

In Denmark with a Fender Competition Mustang bass.

Pla
Da
Ple

In the studio with a Rickenbacker bass, 1970. There's a little bit of McCartney in almost anything every rock bassist has done since the Beatles.

GK: Again, it's back to the blues with the Stones, isn't it? Bill Wyman is drawing a direct line back to Dixon and those walking bass lines on those Chess singles in the early to mid-Fifties. Dixon wasn't a showy bass player either, but those were defining bass lines for those songs. Bill enjoyed being a part of the rhythm section, and Keith totally appreciated the role that he and Charlie played. He called those guys the "Engine Room," and the band doesn't move without the Engine Room operating at top level. I think people notice a difference now with Darryl Jones in the band. He's excellent, but he's a much flashier player than Bill ever was. There is

a difference in the way the band sounds, and it's frankly not as good. It doesn't swing.

JD: No, it doesn't. Part of Wyman's charm was that, like Watts, he was such a stoic presence. You always got the sense that a hurricane could blow across the stage—or a riot, as in the case of Altamont—and absolutely nothing was going to throw Charlie off the beat or get Wyman to move or smile. Those were valuable things when you have Keith Richards and Jagger up front. But McCartney—look at the way he moves on stage or how he leans into the microphone to do a harmony: He's

1969

Novelist and social reformer Upton Sinclair dies, age 90.

Nov. 25

Stones release *Beggars Banquet*.

Dec. 6

Australian media baron Rupert Murdoch purchases largest-selling British Sunday newspaper, *The News of the World*.

Jan. 1

Police at Newark Airport in New Jersey confiscate 30,000 copies of *Two Virgins*

Jan. 3

New York Jets quarterback Joe Namath guarantees victory in Super Bowl III.

Jan. 9

Led Zeppelin release eponymous debut.

Jan. 12

Beatles release *Yellow Submarine* in U.S.

Jan. 13

Beatles begin tumultuous recording sessions for *Let It Be*.

Jan. 22

On the roof of Apple Records building in London, Beatles give last performance.

Jan. 30

Jones found dead in his swimming pool, age 27.

July 3

Stones release "Honky Tonk Women" b/w "You Can't Always Get What You Want" in U.K.

July 4

Stones take stage in front of 250,000 at London's Hyde Park, dedicate their performance to Jones.

July 5

U.S. begins first troop withdrawals from Vietnam.

July 8

Edward Kennedy drives off bridge returning from party on Chappaquiddick Island, Massachusetts.

July 18

Manson family murder Sharon Tate and several friends at home in L.A.; the next night, they murder Rosemary and Leno LaBianca.

Aug. 9

"Three days of peace and music" begin at Woodstock Festival in upstate New York.

Aug. 15

All four Beatles in studio together for last time to finish work on *Abbey Road*.

Aug. 20

Under pseudonym "J," Joan Garrity publishes *The Sensuous Woman*.

Sep.

Jury finds Chicago Seven not guilty of conspiring to incite a riot during protests at 1968 Democratic National Convention.

Feb. 18

Beatles release "Let It Be" b/w "You Know My Name (Look up the Number)" in U.K.; three Weathermen killed while making bomb intended for a military dance in New Jersey.

Mar. 6

Crosby, Stills, Nash & Young, referred to as "the American Beatles" by some, release *Déjà Vu*.

Mar. 11

U.S. Army charges 14 officers with suppressing information related to My Lai massacre.

Mar.17

Phil Spector begins work on *Let It Be*.

Mar. 23

Pres. Nixon signs Public Health Cigarette Smoking Act, banning TV ads starting Jan. 1, 1971.

Apr. 1

Spector finishes work on *Let It Be*.

Apr. 2

Four students at Kent State in Ohio killed by Ohio State National Guard.

May 4

Beatles release *Let It Be* in U.K.

May 8

197

Stones release "Wild Horses" b/w "Sway" in U.S.

June 12

New York Times begins publishing Pentagon Papers.

June 13

First Glastonbury Festival opens in U.K.

June 20

Jim Morrison found dead in his bathtub in Paris, age 27.

July 3

McCartney announces formation of Wings.

Aug. 3

Stones finish recording *Exile on Main St.*

Sep.

Lennon releases *Imagine*.

Sep. 9

Hunter S. Thompson publishes *Fear and Loathing in Las Vegas*.

Nov. 11

Pres. Nixon orders development of space shuttle program.

Jan. 5

67

Stones release "Let's Spend the Night Together" b/w "Ruby Tuesday" in U.S.

Jan. 14

After arguments with *The Ed Sullivan Show* executives, Stones agree to change "Let's Spend the Night Together" to "Let's Spend Some Time Together"; Green Bay Packers defeat Kansas City Chiefs in first Super Bowl.

Jan. 15

Beatles begin recording *Sgt. Pepper's Lonely Hearts Club Band* at Abbey Road.

Jan. 19

Stones release *Between the Buttons* in U.K.

Jan. 20

U.S. sets hourly minimum wage at $1.40.

Feb. 1

Police raid Richards' country estate in Sussex, England; Richards and Jagger charged with drug possession.

Feb. 12

Beatles release "Strawberry Fields Forever" b/w "Penny Lane" in U.S.

Feb. 13

First law prohibiting bootleg recordings enacted in U.S.

Feb. 15

© Aleksandrs Jermakovichs/Shutterstock

Four days of rioting begin in Newark, New Jersey, claiming lives of 27 people.

July 13

Week of rioting begins in Detroit, leaving 40 dead, 2,000 injured, 5,000 homeless.

July 23

Beatles and Epstein lend names to public petition calling for legalization of marijuana in England.

July 24

Fotos International/Hulton Archive/Getty Images

Bonnie and Clyde premieres at Montreal Film Festival.

Aug. 4

Stones release "We Love You" b/w "Dandelion" in U.K.

Aug. 18

Hulton Archive/Getty Images

Beatles attend lecture by Maharishi Mahesh Yogi in London; Abbie Hoffman and Yippies toss fistfuls of paper money onto floor of New York Stock Exchange.

Aug. 24

Epstein found dead in London home, age 32.

Harry Benson/Hulton Archive/Getty Images

Aug. 27

Charles Manson records album *Lie* with Dennis Wilson of Beach Boys producing.

Sep. 11

Tet Offensive halted; South Vietnam recaptures Hué.

Feb. 24

Frankie Lymon found dead from heroin overdose in Harlem, age 25.

Feb. 27

Ronald S. Haeberle/Time & Life Pictures/Getty Images

Stones begin recording *Beggars Banquet* at Olympic Studios.

Mar.

Beatles release "Lady Madonna" b/w "The Inner Light" in U.K.

Mar. 15

American troops kill scores of civilians in what will become known as the My Lai massacre; Robert Kennedy enters race for Democratic presidential nomination.

Mar. 16

Peaceful antiwar protest in London followed by riot outside U.S. Embassy; more than 80 injured.

Mar. 17

Pres. Johnson announces he will not seek reelection.

Mar. 31

2001: A Space Odyssey premieres, Washington, D.C.

Apr. 2

---

150 women arrive in Atlantic City, New Jersey, to protest Miss America Pageant.

Sep. 7

U.S. Department of Defense announces 24,000 troops to be sent back to Vietnam for involuntary second tours of duty.

Oct. 14

U.S. sprinters Tommie Smith and John Carlos expelled from Olympic Games in Mexico City for delivering "Black Power salute" on medal podium.

Rolls Press/Popperfoto/Getty Images

Oct. 16

Beatles finish work on White Album.

Oct. 17

Nixon wins presidency.

Nov. 4

Lennon and Yoko Ono release *Unfinished Music No. 1: Two Virgins* in U.S.

Hulton Archive/Getty Images

Nov. 11

Yale University announces it will admit women; thousands of young Americans burn draft cards as death toll in Vietnam approaches 30,000 and U.S. troop strength reaches peak of 555,000.

Nov. 14

The Beatles, a.k.a. the White Album, released in U.K.

Nov. 22

Oct. 6 — LSD made illegal in U.S.

Nov. — Stones begin spending rest of year at Olympic Studios, London, recording *Between the Buttons*.

Nov. 8 — Ronald Reagan elected governor of California.

Nov. 24 — Beatles begin recording "Strawberry Fields Forever" at Abbey Road.

Dec. 9 — *A Collection of Beatles Oldies* released in U.K.

Dec. 15 — Walt Disney dies in L.A.

Dec. 18 — Animated TV special *How the Grinch Stole Christmas* premieres.

Dec. 29 — Beatles begin recording "Penny Lane" at Abbey Road.

Jan. 10 — U.S. Senate seats Edward W. Brooke, Massachusetts Republican and first black elected to body by popular vote.

June 2 — Race riots shake Roxbury section of Boston.

June 7 — Haight-Ashbury Free Medical Clinic opens in San Francisco.

June 12 — U.S. Supreme Court strikes down state laws prohibiting interracial marriages.

June 13 — Pres. Johnson nominates Thurgood Marshall to become first black U.S. Supreme Court justice.

June 16 — Three-day International Pop Festival begins in Monterey, California.

June 19 — McCartney appears on TV and talks about taking LSD.

June 25 — Beatles record "All You Need is Love" during live TV broadcast watched by estimated 400 million people; Jagger, Faithfull, Richards, Keith Moon, Eric Clapton, Graham Nash are among those singing along in studio audience.

BIPS/Hulton Archive/Getty Images

June 30 — The Who rush release covers of "The Last Time" b/w "Under My Thumb" as show of support during Jagger and Richard's legal troubles.

July 7 — Beatles release "All You Need Is Love" b/w "Baby, You're A Rich Man" in U.S.; jazz giant John Coltrane dies in Huntington, New York, age 40.

1968

Dec. 23 — Stones release "She's a Rainbow" b/w "2000 Light Years from Home."

Jan. 19 — Singer/actress Eartha Kitt denounces the Vietnam War to Lady Bird Johnson while attending a "ladies' lunch" at White House.

AFP/Getty Images

Jan. 30 — Viet Cong forces launch Tet Offensive across South Vietnam.

Jan. 31 — Viet Cong soldiers attack U.S. Embassy in Saigon.

Feb. — Gore Vidal publishes *Myra Breckinridge*.

Feb. 1 — Viet Cong officer executed by South Vietnam official as Eddie Adam captures event in Pulitzer Prize–winning photo; Nixon announces bid for Republican presidential nomination.

Feb. 8 — Three college students killed as South Carolina highway patrolmen break up civil rights protest at whites-only bowling alley in Orangeburg.

Feb. 15 — Beatles travel to Rishikesh, India, to study transcendental meditation under Maharishi Mahesh Yogi.

Robert Lerner/Hulton Archive/Getty Images

Feb. 19 — *Mister Rogers' Neighborhood* premieres.

CBS Photo Archive/Hulton Archive/Getty Images

June 5 — Robert Kennedy shot by Sirhan Sirhan at Ambassador Hotel in L.A.

Hulton Archive/Getty Images

June 13 — Johnny Cash performs at Folsom Prison; Chief Justice Earl Warren submits resignation.

GAB Archive/Redferns/Getty Images

July 17 — Animated film *Yellow Submarine* premieres at London Pavilion.

July 25 — Pope Paul VI publishes *Humanae Vitae*, condemning use of birth control.

APA/Hulton Archive/Getty Images

Aug. 22 — Police clash with antiwar protesters in Chicago outside 1968 Democratic National Convention; Starr leaves Beatles as tension mounts at Abbey Road.

Aug. 26 — Beatles release "Hey Jude" b/w "Revolution" in U.S.

Aug. 29 — Arthur Ashe wins the inaugural U.S. Open tennis tournament.

Aug. 31 — Stones release "Street Fighting Man" b/w "No Expectations" in U.S.

Sep. 5 — Starr rejoins Beatles at Abbey Road.

Popperfoto/Getty Images

U.S. Supreme Court expands students' First Amendment rights.
Feb. 24

Mario Puzo publishes *The Godfather*.
Mar. 10

Lennon and Ono start seven-day "bed-in" at Hilton in Amsterdam.
Mar. 25

Former President Dwight D. Eisenhower dies, age 78.
Mar. 28

300 students seize Harvard University administration building.
Apr. 9

Beatles release "Get Back" b/w "Don't Let Me Down" in U.K.
Apr. 11

Boston Celtics defeat L.A. Lakers to claim their ninth NBA championship of decade.
May 5

McCartney refuses to sign contract appointing Allen Klein business manager for several Beatles companies.
May 8

BBC orders 13 episodes of *Monty Python's Flying Circus*.
May 23

Lt. William Calley charged with premeditated murder for deaths of 19 Vietnamese civilians at My Lai.
Sep. 5

Tom Hanley/Redferns/Getty Images

Lennon quits Beatles.
Sep. 13

Abbey Road released in U.K.
Sep. 26

Beatles release "Something" b/w "Come Together" in U.S.
Oct. 6

Leonard Chess, founder of Chess Records, dies of heart attack, age 52; "Miracle Mets" win World Series at Shea Stadium, New York.
Oct. 16

Hulton Archive/Getty Images

Novelist Jack Kerouac dies in St. Petersburg, Florida, age 47, from cirrhosis.
Oct. 21

Children's Television Archive/Hulton Archive/Getty Images

Sesame Street premieres.
Nov. 10

Protesters in Washington, D.C., stage peaceful demonstration against Vietnam War, including a symbolic "March against Death."
Nov. 15

Lennon returns his MBE to the Queen.
Nov. 25

Beatles release "The Long and Winding Road" b/w "For You Blue" in U.S.
May 11

Pres. Nixon signs measure lowering voting age to 18.
June 10

U.S. ground troops withdraw from Cambodia.
June 28

Jeffrey Mayer/WireImage/Getty Images

Isle of Wight Festival begins off coast of England.
Aug. 26

Bentley Archive/Popperfoto/Getty Images

Jimi Hendrix dies in London, age 27, from causes never officially identified.
Sep. 18

Stones finish recording *Sticky Fingers*.
Oct.

Michael Ochs Archives/Getty Images

Janis Joplin found dead from a drug overdose, age 27.
Oct. 4

Pres. Nixon announces U.S. to withdraw 40,000 troops from Vietnam before Christmas.
Oct. 12

Pittsburgh Pirates defeat the Baltimore Orioles 4–3 in World Series' first-ever scheduled night game.
Oct. 13

72

Getty Images

On "Bloody Sunday," British Army kills 14 unarmed civil rights marchers in Derry, Northern Ireland.
Jan. 30

Anti-British riots take place throughout Ireland; *A Clockwork Orange* released in U.S.
Feb. 2

Pres. Nixon begins unprecedented 8-day visit to China.
Feb. 21

Movie adaptation of *The Godfather* released in U.S.
Mar. 24

Stones release "Tumbling Dice" b/w "Sweet Black Angel" in U.S.
Apr. 15

Stones release *Exile on Main St.*
May 12

Gov. Wallace of Alabama is shot.
May 15

Stones commence infamous 48-date 1972 North American tour in Vancouver.
June 3

White House operatives arrested for burglarizing Democratic Party offices at Watergate Hotel.
June 17

1966

Richard Speck murders 8 student nurses in Chicago dormitory.
July 14

Dylan crashes motorcycle near his home in Woodstock, New York.
July 29

England captures FIFA World Cup, besting West Germany 4-2 at Wembley Stadium.
July 30

Lenny Bruce dies of morphine overdose, age 41.
Aug. 3

Brian Epstein holds press conference to explain Lennon's "Jesus" quote.
Aug. 6

Beatles release *Revolver* and "Eleanor Rigby" b/w "Yellow Submarine" in U.S.
Aug. 8

Star Trek premieres on NBC.
Sep. 8

Stones release "Have You Seen Your Mother, Baby, Standing in the Shadow?" b/w "Who's Driving Your Plane?" in U.S.
Sep. 24

Nazi war criminals Albert Speer and Baldur von Schirach freed after serving 20-year sentences.
Sep. 30

Physicist Robert Oppenheimer, driving force behind development of atomic bomb, dies at 62.
Feb. 18

Svetlana Alliluyeva, daughter of Josef Stalin, appears at U.S. Embassy in India to announce her defection to West.
Mar. 6

The Velvet Underground & Nico released.
Mar. 12

Beatles finish recording *Sgt. Pepper's Lonely Hearts Club Band*.
Apr. 21

Beatles begin recording songs for *Magical Mystery Tour* and others that will end up on *Yellow Submarine*.
Apr. 25

Muhammad Ali stripped of heavyweight title for refusing to serve in U.S. Army on religious grounds.
Apr. 28

Lennon takes delivery of Rolls-Royce with psychedelic paint job.
May 25

Stones begin recording *Their Satanic Majesties Request* at Olympic Studios, intermittently continuing throughout summer between drug busts, court appearances, Oldham's resignation.
June

Beatles release *Sgt. Pepper's Lonely Hearts Club Band* in U.S.
June 2

Protest in Madison, Wisconsin, against recruiting by Dow Chemical, maker of napalm and Agent Orange, turns violent.
Oct. 18

Pres. Johnson signs bill establishing Corporation for Public Broadcasting.
Nov. 7

Rolling Stone magazine, cofounded by Jann Wenner in San Francisco, publishes debut issue with press run of 40,000 copies.
Nov. 9

Beatles finish work on songs for *Magical Mystery Tour*.
Nov. 15

Beatles release "Hello, Goodbye" b/w "I Am the Walrus" in U.K.
Nov. 24

Beatles release *Magical Mystery Tour*.
Nov. 27

Stones release *Their Satanic Majesties Request*.
Dec. 8

Otis Redding and six others die when private plane crashes in Wisconsin.
Dec. 10

The Graduate premieres.
Dec. 20

Martin Luther King Jr. assassinated in Memphis, Tennessee; riots erupt in American cities.
Apr. 4

Pres. Johnson signs Civil Rights Act of 1968.
Apr. 11

Students at Columbia University in New York City take over administration buildings and shut down campus for week.
Apr. 23

Hair opens on Broadway.
Apr. 29

Stones release "Jumpin' Jack Flash" b/w "Child of the Moon" in U.K.
May 24

Back from India, Beatles begin work on self-titled recording to become known as the White Album, alternating between Abbey Road and Trident studios.
May 30

Stones finish recording *Beggars Banquet*.
June

Helen Keller dies, age 87.
June 1

Andy Warhol shot by Valerie Solanis at his studio, the Factory.
June 3

United Artists/Hulton Archive/Getty Images

Michael Putland/Hulton Archive/Getty Images

Midnight Cowboy released in U.S.

May 25

Lennon and Ono stage another "bed-in" in Montreal.

May 26

Beatles release "The Ballad of John and Yoko" b/w "Old Brown Shoe" in U.K.

May 30

Stones announce Brian Jones has left band.

June 8

Stones hire Mick Taylor; continue recording sessions for *Let It Bleed* at Olympic Studios, begun in late 1968.

June 12

Warren E. Burger sworn in as Chief Justice of U.S. Supreme Court.

June 23

Stonewall riots in New York City mark start of modern gay rights movement in U.S.

June 28

Beatles begin recording *Abbey Road*.

July 2

Robert Altman/Michael Ochs Archives/Getty Images

1970

Stones release *Let It Bleed* in U.S.

Nov. 29

Stones begin recording *Sticky Fingers* at Muscle Shoals Studios, Alabama.

Dec. 1

Black Panther Party members Fred Hampton and Mark Clark shot dead in their sleep during raid by Chicago police officers.

Dec. 4

Stones play Altamont Speedway; 18-year-old Meredith Hunter killed by Hells Angels as band performs "Under My Thumb."

Dec. 6

Jackson 5 appear on the *Ed Sullivan Show*.

Dec. 14

Jagger fined £200 for possession of cannabis.

Jan. 26

Bluesman Slim Harpo dies of heart attack, age 46. (Stones will cover Harpo's "Shake Your Hips" as "Hip Shake" on *Exile on Main St..)*

Jan. 31

Erich Segal publishes *Love Story*.

Feb. 14

Tom Hanley/Redferns/Getty Images

Michael Ochs Archives/Getty Images

1971

Garry Trudeau's *Doonesbury* debuts in about two dozen U.S. newspapers.

Oct. 26

Harrison releases *All Things Must Pass.*

Nov. 27

Manson and three others found guilty of Tate-LaBianca murders.

Jan. 25

William Peter Blatty publishes *The Exorcist.*

Feb.

Stones release "Brown Sugar" b/w "Bitch" in U.K.

Apr. 16

Stones release *Sticky Fingers* in U.K.

Apr. 23

Thomas Harris publishes *I'm O.K., You're O.K.*; Stones begin recording *Exile on Main St.* at Nellcôte in France.

May

Vietnam Veterans for a Just Peace speak out against war protests.

June 1

Marty Temme/Wireimage/Getty Images

Staff Photo/AFP/Getty Images

Terry Ashe/Time & Life Pictures/Getty Images

Pres. Nixon and chief of staff, H. R. Haldeman, taped talking about obstructing FBI investigation into Watergate burglary.

June 23

Bluesman Fred McDowell dies, age 68. (Stones covered his "You Gotta Move" on *Sticky Fingers*.)

July 3

Comedian George Carlin arrested in Milwaukee, Wisconsin, for reciting his "Seven Words You Can Never Say on Television."

July 21

11 Israeli athletes murdered by Arab terrorists at Summer Olympics in Munich.

Sep. 5

Team Canada defeats Soviet Union in Game 8 of ice hockey's "Summit Series."

Sep. 28

FBI hires its first female agents.

Oct. 25

Pres. Nixon defeats Democratic challenger Sen. George McGovern in landslide.

Nov. 7

Jonathan Livingston Seagull by Richard Bach is bestselling book of 1972 in U.S.; it will claim same distinction in 1973

Dec. 31

Wyman on the set of *Ready Steady Go!*, October 7, 1966.

always saying, "Look at me, look at me!" Part of it is you can do that in a four-piece band, where in a five-piece or larger group, there's less space. That's another way that Wyman was the perfect bass player for the Stones: He knew that. But, as I said, I think we have to give this one to McCartney. The things he has done on those four strings have influenced every bass player in any rock genre you can name, from Dee Dee Ramone to Tom Araya of Slayer. There is some McCartney in what almost any rock bassist has done since the Beatles.

GK: With McCartney, between the harmony vocals and his bass-playing, he gave the Beatles an orchestral dimension that the Stones never quite matched. Paul brought a sophistication to the Beatles' sound. His bass lines were melodies that complemented the vocal parts.

And his style influenced countless future players, the way he presaged heavy metal and incorporated a bit of funk into his playing on "I Want You," for example. Genius-level stuff.

JD: The main hook in "Come Together" is really his bass-playing.

GK: Yeah! You wouldn't have the song without the bass. But you can even go back to the early songs, like "I Want to Hold Your Hand," and the bass is really holding it together. It is on equal footing with the guitars. Even in a simple ballad like "Michelle," the way his bass counterpoints the guitar chords, the richness and elegance of those melodies have a lot to do with how the bass accents things. So, hands down, McCartney wins.

McCARTNEY

HOW LOW CAN HE GO?

by Greg Kot

"I WANT TO HOLD YOUR HAND" *(1964)*
Even at this early stage, the bass is on equal footing with the guitars, and it rises to the forefront during the bridge.

"MICHELLE" *(1965)*
The opening line counterpoints the descending guitar chords and ushers in one of Paul's most elegant melodies.

"PAPERBACK WRITER" *(1966)*
The bass becomes a lead instrument with the way it rolls out a red carpet of notes for each verse, and McCartney is now playing a role in the band that suggests Liverpool's answer to Motown's James Jamerson.

"RAIN" *(1966)*
Underneath Ringo's massive drumming, McCartney's bass is equally brilliant as it rides up, down, and all around on the heaviest of all Beatles tracks.

"LUCY IN THE SKY WITH DIAMONDS" *(1967)*
Rather than sticking with root chords, the bass plays an independent melody that expertly complements the main line.

"BABY, YOU'RE A RICH MAN" *(1967)*
In anticipation of funk and hip-hop, here's the kind of subterranean tone that lowriders could use to test their speaker systems.

"EVERYBODY'S GOT SOMETHING TO HIDE EXCEPT ME AND MY MONKEY" *(1968)*
Monster heaviness, especially the way McCartney's Godzilla bass stalks Lennon's frantic lead/rhythm guitar until everything is reduced to rubble. For a few seconds Paul's ax has the song all to itself.

"COME TOGETHER" *(1969)*
A sparse yet heavy song, with thick, melodic bass as the dominant instrument.

"I WANT YOU (SHE'S SO HEAVY)" *(1969)*
Another bare-bones Lennon song that allows McCartney to experiment like mad, and he pushes into jazz or heavy funk territory à la Bootsy Collins.

"GOLDEN SLUMBERS"/"CARRY THAT WEIGHT" *(1969)*
The *Abbey Road* album was McCartney's tour de force, and his virtuoso bass lines achieve an orchestral splendor.

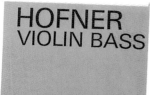

HOFNER VIOLIN BASS

Popularised by Paul McCartney of "Beatles" fame, the Hofner Violin Bass is one of the smallest and lightest hollow-back bass guitars made today. Fitted with double-pole, double-coil "NOVA-SONIC" pick-ups and flick-action switches for instant tone change, this guitar is a favourite with many groups for its powerful, rich tonal quality.

A superb instrument for today's modern players. Attractive brunette sunburst finish.

Body Dimensions : 18" x 11" x 2⅜".

No. 5150 Violin Bass .. 58 Gns.

No. 5965 Rich felt-lined
shaped case for
above .. .. 10 Gns.

Cases, see page 53.

Page Thirty-five

130

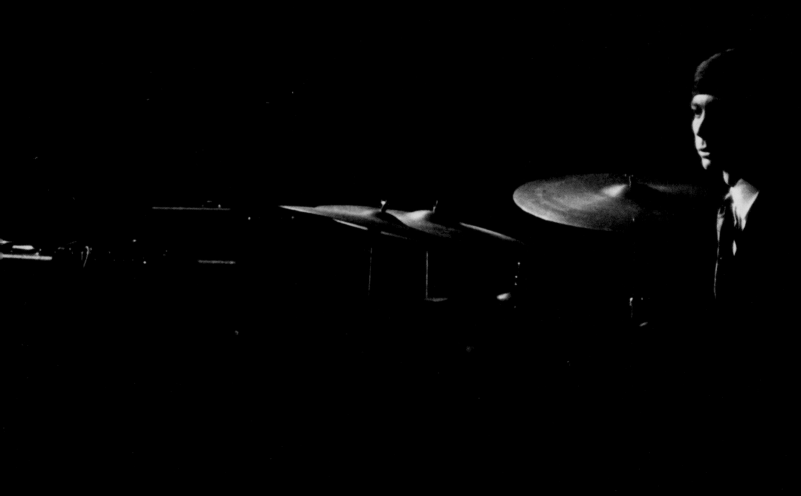

GIVE THE DRUMMERS SOME

CHARLIE AND RINGO

Starr with Rory Storm & the Hurricanes, St. Luke's Church Hall, North Liverpool, August 1961.
From left: Rory Storm (Alan Caldwell), Johnny Guitar (Johnny Byrne), Starr, and Lu Walters (Wally Eymond).

KAISERKELLER
Tanzpalast der Jugend
HAMBURG - ST. PAULI
FESTIVAL DER ROCK'n ROLL FANS

IM MONAT OCTOBER - NOVEMBER - DEZEMBER

Präsentiert Bruno Koschmider

ORIGINAL
Rock'n Roll
BANDS

Rory Storm
AND HIS
HVRICAN
und
The Beatles
ENGLAND - LIVERPOOL

JD: It's time for our last Beatle vs. Stone cage match, between the drummers of these two bands. And I have a feeling we're going to have more to say about Charlie Watts and Ringo Starr than the other instrumentalists because they both were very important to these groups above and beyond their musical contributions.

GK: When you think about how Charlie and Ringo have been assessed over time, they rarely get the credit they deserve. They are never really mentioned as two of the greatest drummers in rock history; you always hear the guys with the big kits or the flamboyant technique mentioned ahead of them, while Charlie and Ringo usually are mentioned only because they are parts of two of the biggest rock bands ever. I don't think they have gotten the credit for being innovators or for their indispensable roles in creating some of the best rock songs ever.

A lifelong jazz disciple, Watts (background) got his R&B education with Cyril Davies. They're seen here, pre-Stones, at the Marquee Club, London, 1962.

GRAFTON BALLROOM
THURSDAY, JANUARY 10th
7-30————12-30
FIRST MERSEYSIDE APPEARANCE IN 1963 OF
THE BEATLES
with GERRY AND THE PACEMAKERS
SONNY WEBB AND THE CASCADES
THE JOHNNY HILTON SHOW BAND
THE BILLY ELLIS TRIO
M.C.1 BOB WOOLER
TICKETS 7/-   In Advance 6 -
FROM NEMS. RUSHWORTH'S. LEWIS'S. CRANE'S. HESSY'S
AND THE GRAFTON

Starr, 1963, and Watts, 1964.

HARRINGAY JAZZ CLUB
"THE MANOR HOUSE" (Opp. Manor House Tube)
★ NANDA and RON LESLEY present ★
RHYTHM AND BLUES
THURSDAY, 14th FEBRUARY.
8—11 p.m.
with **THE BLUES BY SIX**
featuring BRIAN KNIGHT PLUS
THE ROLLING STONES
Members 4/-. Harringay Jazz Club Membership Valid
FREE Membership Tonight.   HI-FI, plus Watneys Red Barrel !

The "goofy Beatle" during filming of *Help!*, 1965.

JD: I have two theories. One is that Ringo and Charlie are personalities: They are characters. Rightly or wrongly, they were shoehorned into particular roles in each of their bands, both of which became larger than life. Two, as musicians with distinctive styles, they were dedicated first and foremost to playing the songs. That's a quality in rock 'n' roll musicians that is often underappreciated. It happens with bass players too, but drummers get it even more.

Let's talk about the personalities first. The fact that these guys are such memorable characters sometimes overshadows their very significant musical contributions. Ringo, of course, was set up to be "the goofy Beatle." If Paul was the heartthrob, George was the quiet and mysterious one, and Lennon was the brains, Ringo was the goofball. Just look at the movies: In *A Hard Day's*

Night, he wanders off on his own, and he's a sad sack who causes all this comedic trouble. The title itself is one of his famous malapropisms; he was always mangling things in a funny way. Then, in *Help!*, he's even wackier—a sort of low-rent Peter Sellers. Meanwhile, on the albums, Ringo is grudgingly given the silliest songs to sing, the most cartoon-like material: "Yellow Submarine" or "With a Little Help from My Friends." And the latter is really an insult: This guy tries but fails, and he can only get by with a little help from his more talented pals!

Charlie is a less silly or downtrodden character, but he's distinctive in a different way. First off, he's this Cro-Magnon-looking dude. Plus, he's aloof and a little enigmatic, but he always has his dignity. Famously, in *The True Adventures of the Rolling Stones*, Stanley Booth calls him "The world's politest man."

Watts and "his singer" on the set of *Ready Steady Go!*, London, June 26, 1964. Richards has said the Stones are Watts' band: "When Charlie quits, the Stones are over."

Everyone in the Stones' camp loves to tell Charlie stories. The classic, perhaps apocryphal, holds that in the mid-Eighties, a drunken Mick Jagger phoned Charlie's hotel room in the middle of the night asking where "his drummer" was. Watts allegedly rose, shaved, dressed in his suit and tie and perfectly polished loafers, walked over to Jagger's room, punched him in the nose, and said, "Don't ever call me your drummer again. You're *my* fucking singer!"

GK: Doesn't the story go that he knocked Jagger into a plate of smoked salmon?

JD: Who knows? As I said, it might not have happened at all. But it's such a perfect story, it *should* have happened!

Now, I've interviewed both of these drumming heroes, and Charlie *is* the politest man in the world—there's a certain upper-class, English, aristocratic grace about him. He's a man of very few words. He's obviously very intelligent, yet you also get the distinct impression that you'd really better not mess with him! I've talked to Ringo too, and he's naturally charming and very endearing, if a little smarmy at times. However, in both cases, the personalities shouldn't overshadow what they did behind those drum sets.

Both Watts and Starr are underestimated in general, but particularly for the textures they brought to their respective bands' songs.

GK: You take a look at these guys, and you get a mental image of what they contribute to the band musically, and that's not always an accurate way to judge anyone. The image of Ringo is always the Muppet in the back with the huge grin on his face. No matter what was going on, he was always smiling and wagging his head. He seemed to be having a ball, without a care in the world—as if he didn't have a single thought going through his mop-topped head aside from banging on things. And I do remember seeing the back cover of the Rolling Stones' *Hot Rocks* in my youth and thinking, "This guy Charlie is the most intriguing, scariest guy in this band, just by the way he looks." Then you see him drumming with that very erect posture, his hands barely seeming to move, and you realize he's the exact opposite of these flamboyant Sixties rock drummers like Keith Moon, Ginger Baker, or John Bonham.

Ringo defined the joy of rock 'n' roll and the idea of what a drummer should look like in a rock 'n' roll band. Charlie, on the other hand, seems to belong to another world, the jazz world. That posture is like Kenny Clarke's—it has nothing to do with wild-ass rock 'n' roll. And it's all in the wrists! Those hands never come above the shoulders, barely move above the waist, and yet he produces this crushing snare-drum sound.

JD: The most obvious drummer-muso difference between the two is that Ringo championed the matched grip, which became the standard in rock, while Charlie always stuck with the traditional grip, just like most jazz drummers to this day.

GK: Charlie worshipped those jazz drummers and continued playing their music in his side projects

throughout the Stones' career. How he ended up in a rock 'n' roll band of this magnitude and size—I think he probably asks himself that question once in a while!

JD: Well, I think Charlie's jazz roots are sometimes overstated. I know his labor of love is to go out and drive a big jazz band. Obviously, he's steeped in that music, and he knows and loves it. I know you've seen the book he did as a young illustrator, *Ode to a High Flying Bird*, that really charming cartoon account of the life of Charlie Parker. And Charlie Watts certainly took his fashion cues from the bebop era. But make no mistake: He is a *rock* drummer. The jazz creeps in at times—mostly in his own version of that famous Bernard Purdie shuffle—but for the most part, Charlie is all about the backbeat on two and four, albeit in that slightly behind-the-beat way that a lot of British rock drummers play.

Ringo has a bit of that laidback feel too, though he's coming much more from the American school of rockabilly and country—Jerry Lee Lewis and Chet Atkins.

As evidenced by his hallmark traditional grip, seen here on the set of *Ready Steady Go!*, Watts worshiped jazz drummers and continued in the genre with his side projects throughout the Stones' career.

Opposite: Champion of the matched grip, Starr defined the joy of rock 'n' roll and the idea of what a drummer in a rock band should look like.

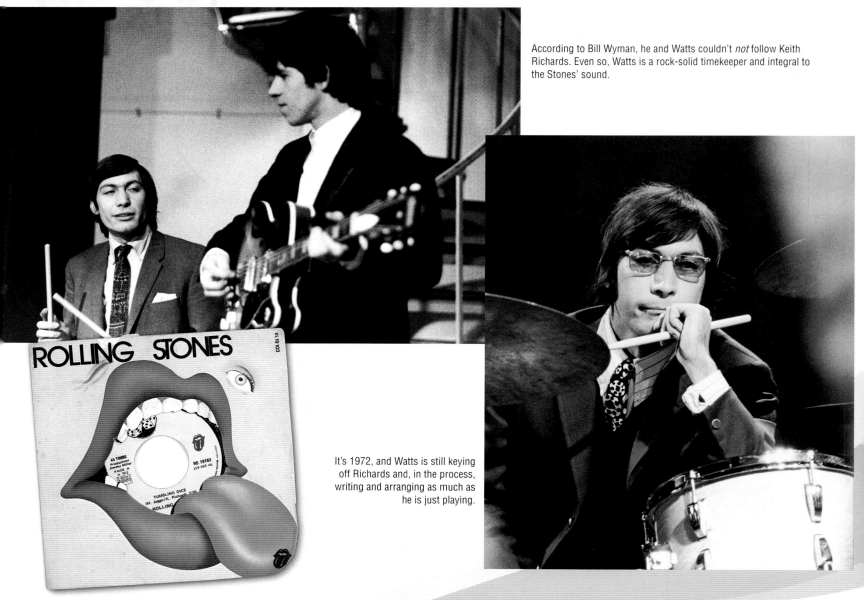

According to Bill Wyman, he and Watts couldn't *not* follow Keith Richards. Even so, Watts is a rock-solid timekeeper and integral to the Stones' sound.

ROLLING STONES

It's 1972, and Watts is still keying off Richards and, in the process, writing and arranging as much as he is just playing.

GK: Maybe you as a drummer can address this: The one thing drummers always point out about Charlie is that technically, he's an oddity, in that he hits the snare at a different time than the hi-hat. They aren't in sync. Do you make anything of that?

JD: That's the behind-the-beat thing I was talking about, like a slight hesitancy. With Charlie, and to some extent with Ringo, it often feels as if they're pulling the rhythm rather than pushing it right on top of the beat in the American way. But both are just rock-solid as timekeepers. I mean, Charlie sometimes speeds up and slows down, even on record, but it's always in the interest of matching the emotions of the song. As for Ringo, they say he was so consistent in the studio that the band could do fifty takes of a song and his time wouldn't vary at all from take number one to take number forty-nine.

Neither of these drummers gets the credit he deserves for subtle touches. Ringo will put his stick flat on the drumhead and play the rim on the backbeat, say,

and it's just a very little musical difference, this rimshot, but it has a big effect on the whole song. They both do a whole lot with very little. Part of it is that people who don't really understand drumming look at them and say, "Those guys have one mounted tom and one floor tom each—they're playing these really tiny kits, so they can't be very good," as opposed to the heavy-metal or progressive-rock drummers who followed with sixty drums and cymbals! In fact, the best drummers can sit behind a four-piece set and do everything that a flashier musician can do, and, if anything, it's more challenging to do it on a smaller instrument.

As for Ringo's chops, listen to a song like "Rain," which is just an incredibly complicated drum track. It's very, very busy and full of these complex drum fills that actually propel rather than just decorate the song. If Tony Williams, Billy Cobham, Carmine Appice, or someone like that had played it on a big, flashy drum set, people would have said, "Wow, that's progressive-rock drumming at its best!"

Starr wasn't just playing the drums—he was orchestrating the emotions.

GK: The drumming on "Rain" qualifies as heavy metal, years before Black Sabbath got credit for inventing it. Even going back to the early Beatles tracks, the drumming played a huge role in defining this new sound from England. On "She Loves You," it's jaw-dropping how massive the drums sound on that track. If you go back to the stuff that preceded it in rock 'n' roll, there was nothing quite like the sound of Ringo's tom-toms. Then he'd move into that sizzle attack on the hi-hat, and it would really raise the temperature, the excitement level, of the song. He wasn't just playing the drums—he was orchestrating the emotions.

JD: That's what I'm saying about subtlety. Both of these musicians have a way of playing exactly what the song needs, whether it's something complex or a part that's incredibly simple but soulful. Listen to the beginning of "Honky Tonk Women" and the short intro with Charlie's

drums in tandem with producer Jimmy Miller's cowbell. It's the perfect thing to usher in that song.

GK: That *is* the song right there! He and Miller basically wrote the song with that intro. They should have gotten the co-songwriting credit on that.

JD: Absolutely. Or look at the way "Sympathy for the Devil" comes together in the studio around Charlie and Bill Wyman. Jean-Luc Godard captured that on film, where you actually see that song come together. It's going nowhere at first, just a flat jam in the studio, until Charlie happens upon this kind of slowed-down, inside-out, Bo Diddley or Bernard Purdie shuffle, and all of a sudden that song becomes something. It's a masterpiece, and it didn't work until he found the right groove for it.

The happy-go-lucky personality needed to hold together the other colliding talents in the Beatles? Budokan, Tokyo, June 30, 1966.

GK: Keith has said emphatically that the Stones are basically Charlie's band: "When Charlie quits, the Stones are over." That is an interesting thing to say about a drummer. I wish the Who would have said the same thing about Keith Moon.

When I watch the Stones live now, even though they have become a self-parody playing the same songs over and over in stadiums for top-dollar ticket prices, the one thing I notice is the way Keith's guitar works off of Charlie's drums. That is the key relationship in the Stones. Rhythmically, the way Keith and Charlie work together defines them as a band. You can hear that interplay in songs like "Brown Sugar," "Tumbling Dice," or "Bitch"—Charlie's drumming keys off Keith's guitar-playing to create the feel, the atmosphere, and the foundation for the song to unfold. Everything else falls in with what those two guys are doing. That, to my mind, is Watts writing and arranging a song as much as he is playing it.

I agree that he also doesn't get enough credit for the subtleties in his style. Yes, he is in many ways a quintessential rock drummer, but then there's "Moonlight Mile," a rapturous display where he's using mallets to create a wash of melancholy and longing that ties in directly with the lyrics.

JD: What you said about Charlie and Keith being key to the music, it is also true about the chemistries in these bands. There is endless armchair psychoanalysis about how the Stones and the Beatles worked as creative units, but I don't think you can forget that question of personality that we started with. When you have Lennon and McCartney in this intense competition to outdo one another, with Harrison on the side as the frustrated but brilliant songwriter just trying to get a track on the album, an eager, charming, happy-go-lucky personality like Ringo probably was needed just to bring these other colliding talents together.

Watts often has been described as a stabilizing influence and an incredibly classy guy in a band where everyone was always spinning off into the wasteland. Forest Hills, Queens, New York, July 2, 1966.

GK: He's definitely the glue in that band. I think that's what Keith means when he says, "The Stones fall apart when Charlie leaves." He basically let Charlie pick Bill Wyman's replacement in the Nineties. Not Mick, not Keith, not poor Ronnie Wood—it was up to Charlie. It became Darryl Jones because Charlie said, "That's the guy."

Ditto about Ringo. Think about it: When they all went on to make solo albums, who was the one common element in all of their work? Ringo. He was the guy who played drums for all of them post-Beatles. He was the one guy in the room they wanted to be around and felt comfortable working with. When the Beatles started falling apart during recording of the White Album, the low point was when Ringo felt unloved and unwanted and he actually left the band for a brief stint. That's when you realized these guys were not going to make

it, because if Ringo couldn't get along with them, then no one could.

JD: These guys were the heart and soul in both of their bands, not only musically, but spiritually. Tough to pick a winner here: Ringo or Charlie? Who wins for you?

GK: The conventional wisdom says Charlie wins, but if you pull apart those Beatles songs, Ringo's drumming is essential. I can't imagine either one of those bands going on without either of those guys. It has to be a tie.

JD: We're not copping out here, it's just that either would be horrified at the fact that we were even going to debate this because they are supporting players in the best sense of that word, and that's what great rock 'n' roll is built on. They both gave exactly what those bands needed.

CHARLIE AND RINGO

IN THE POCKET

by Jim DeRogatis

Here are some of the best musical moments from Charlie Watts and Ringo Starr.

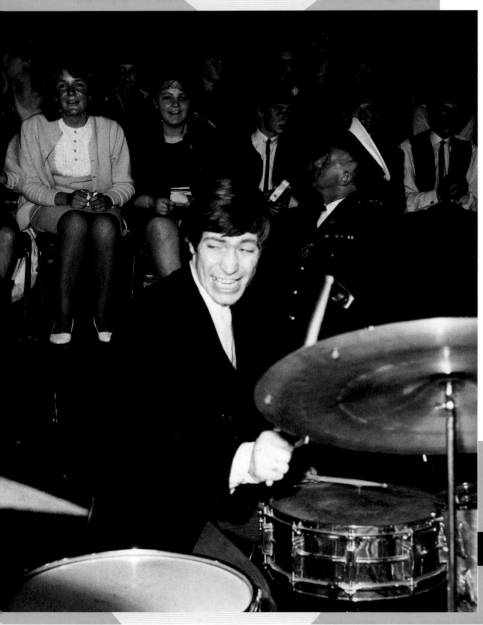

CHARLIE WATTS

"HONKY TONK WOMEN" *(1969)*
You've just got to love the stumbling drum intro and shaky but fundamentally solid and vaguely Latin groove, which very much evokes that gin-soaked barroom queen strutting her stuff in Memphis.

"YOU CAN'T ALWAYS GET WHAT YOU WANT" *(1969)*
Charlie's drum fills make the song, adding the necessary drama and grandeur, and building on classic swing triplets.

"BROWN SUGAR" *(1971)*
Sure, the one-two bass-snare attack *sounds* simple, but Charlie's part is the perfect complement to Keith Richards' guitar riff.

"BITCH" *(1971)*
Again, listen to the way that Charlie, with just a hint of a boogie groove this time, perfectly accents Keith's guitar licks.

"TUMBLING DICE" *(1972)*
He may sound sloppy, hitting the snare and the cymbal slightly off-kilter and out of time, but it's all in the service of conjuring those rolling dice that Mick Jagger is singing about, and, in the end, it's absolutely perfect.

RINGO STARR

"TICKET TO RIDE" *(1964)*
A unique groove that defines forward momentum, and then Ringo kicks things over the top with his simple but emphatic flams.

"RAIN" *(1966)*
Many consider this psychedelic rock song to be Ringo's finest moment, and it's essentially one long, ever-shifting fill across the tom-toms that somehow, miraculously, never loses the groove.

"TOMORROW NEVER KNOWS" *(1966)*
An early example of a timeless drum loop, a tribal trance groove that essentially is the most melodic element in the song.

"HERE COMES THE SUN" *(1969)*
If you think Ringo was only about playing two and four, listen to the way he smoothly navigates the complicated changes in this song as it moves from 11/8 to 4/4 to 7/8.

"COME TOGETHER" *(1969)*
Merging a sixteenth-note hi-hat flourish with a dramatic drum roll, Ringo not only propels the song but provides its most dramatic moments.

8 AND IN THE END, THE LOVE YOU MAKE... ETC., ETC.

THE LATE SIXTIES AND THE EARLY SEVENTIES

Police hold back fans at the premiere of the film *Yellow Submarine*, London Pavilion, July 17, 1968.

Harrison with a Blue Meanie at a press screening of *Yellow Submarine*, July 8, 1968.

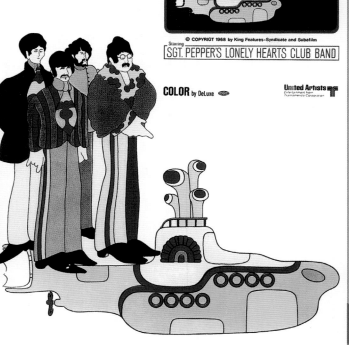

Lennon and Ono's *Unfinished Music No. 1: Two Virgins* must have been an affront to the other Beatles, released as it was a week after the White Album. The album was also an affront to many others because of its sleeve photo, which depicted Lennon and Ono naked and prompted record distributors to wrap it in brown paper.

JD: You made the point earlier, Greg, that once we hit 1968, the Rolling Stones really were ramping up while the Beatles were winding down. I think it's time to look at the end of the Sixties, to compare the final phase of the Beatles with the Stones of the same period.

GK: In this era, a torch is passed. The Beatles are fragmenting and the Stones gather strength.

JD: So, it's June 1968, and the Beatles release *Yellow Submarine*.

GK: Ugh! I was hoping we could ignore it. It's just a pieced-together collection of leftovers to mark time until the White Album came out five months later.

JD: Hey, I kinda like that album! I never liked the movie, but there are some great retro-*Revolver*-style moments of psychedelia on the song half of *Yellow Submarine*. Half of the album is given over to the instrumental score, but on the song side, "Hey Bulldog" is as good as the Beatles ever got in the psychedelic-rock realm. The guitar line is fierce! Sure, "All Together Now" is a complete toss-off, but Harrison has some fine moments with "Only a Northern Song" and "It's All Too Much."

GK: I think you're straining to make a case for a record that doesn't hold up. "All You Need Is Love" feels like a really forced sentiment. Even Lennon, who wrote it, called it a piece of propaganda.

JD: Well, I'm not going to give up on "Hey Bulldog" because it's one of my favorite Beatles songs. Then the White Album comes out in November 1968 and it's a huge seller, but it's a really flawed effort.

GK: The cracks in the armor are already evident. Geoff Emerick, the Beatles' long-time engineer, leaves the White Album sessions because he's tired of the bickering. George Martin takes a vacation while recording is still going on because he feels superfluous. And Ringo quits the band for a few days.

JD: He was the first to quit the Beatles, though that's often forgotten or overlooked.

GK: Then the album comes out in November 1968 and Lennon undercuts it a week later by releasing the first John and Yoko record, *Unfinished Music No. 1: Two Virgins*, the happy couple posing stark naked on the album cover.

JD: That album cover meant a lot to me when I was thirteen!

GK: But can you imagine the affront that was? Can you imagine being the other three Beatles and realizing that John was putting that out at the same time as this album they had spilled blood over? It had to be clear to all of them that the band was no longer a priority, certainly not for Lennon.

Meanwhile, the Stones are emerging from the debacle of '67: the year of drug busts and distractions and the failed psychedelic detour into *Their Satanic Majesties Request*. In 1968, they get back to the business of being the Rolling Stones. Andrew Loog Oldham is out as manager and producer, and they bring in producer Jimmy Miller to work on the single "Jumpin' Jack Flash." That song launches the new era, and it's an emphatic declaration that the Stones are back to being the Stones.

Jones recording *Beggars Banquet*, Olympic Studios, London, July 1968.

JD: Not long after that, Keith bonds with Gram Parsons and the band is more directly experiencing American music and working with American peers from their own generation, which is how they found their true identity. Even though the Stones were trying hard, at some point, probably in the midst of *Satanic Majesties*, they realized they never were going to beat the Beatles in that game of using the recording studio to create new worlds for their listeners. It did prompt some inspired work from them, but that wasn't going to be what they were about. So the question became, "Brian Jones is folding fast; what are we going to be now?"

GK: "Jumpin' Jack Flash" is their answer. You mention these country influences creeping in. In the air at this time we had Dylan's *John Wesley Harding* and *Big*

Pink by the Band and the Byrds' *Sweetheart of the Rodeo*, a country-rock album on which Gram Parsons played a major role. Keith begins experimenting with country guitar tunings and stumbles on a great sound when he plays his acoustic guitar into a cheap cassette recorder and overloads it—that's how the immortal riff for "Jumpin' Jack Flash" was laid down. They segue into their 1968 album *Beggars Banquet*, where Miller is producing his first full-length Stones record. Revolution is in the air—civic unrest in Chicago, Detroit, Birmingham, Paris, and Prague—and the Stones have at it in "Street Fighting Man." Another huge Keith riff, violence in the music, and ambiguity in Jagger's voice: *"But what can a poor boy do/Except to sing for a rock 'n' roll band?"* Revolution is for suckers, according to Mr. Jagger.

Decca and London Records rejected the original intended sleeve art for *Beggars Banquet (above)*. It was reinstated upon the first CD remastering in 1984. The flap delayed the album's 1968 release.

Revolution is for suckers . . . we're just a rock 'n' roll band.

JD: Well, what you could have done in 1968 was put your ass on the line to stand up for something. The MC5 did it here in Chicago; it was the only rock band to show up to play at the Democratic National Convention just as the riots began. And tens of thousands of brave young men and women were making a stand against what they considered to be an unjust war in Vietnam, not to mention myriad other causes, such as sexual inequality and gay rights and the class problems in Britain and the U.S. There was *a lot* that a poor boy could do besides sing for a rock 'n' roll band! And besides, Jagger was far from poor.

Anyway, we're seeing a new costume that these veteran role players are donning. They had done the "young, privileged, white Englishmen pretending we're old, poor, drunken bluesmen" routine, and it had played out. Now they were going to pretend that they were country hillbillies, which, in some ways, particularly with Keith, may have been closer to the heart of what they really were, if not the reality. When he is singing "Salt of the Earth," I believe he means it. You and I have had the privilege of interviewing Keith several times, and I do believe that we could walk with him into any shot-and-a-beer workingman's bar in Chicago or anywhere else in the U.S., in a black neighborhood or a white neighborhood, and it wouldn't be long before everyone in the bar thought he was the greatest guy in the world and started buying him drinks!

GK: At the same time, Jagger's contribution to this seemingly heartfelt Richards lyric about the working class in "Salt of the Earth" is to express his disdain, singing the lines: *"They don't look real to me/In fact they look so strange."* As usual, it's the Stones putting a cynical twist on an "I'd like to teach the world to sing" moment. The Stones are in solidarity with no one except themselves.

As for the blues, "Stray Cat Blues" is as nasty a blues song as they have ever done. It's their response to a song like Sonny Boy Williamson's "Good Morning, School Girl." The Stones bring Sonny Boy's school playground backstage, where they seduce an underage groupie. So much for romance! The Stones were rock's misogynist pigs, and proud of it.

JD: But that is them showing their true selves—their vile, sexist personas without the veneer of pretending to be Muddy Waters.

GK: Exactly. It also played into this idea of the "evil" Stones that a song like "Sympathy for the Devil" tweaked and exploited. In that song, they embrace the label, but they also say, "Hey, wait a minute, we're not the only devils out here. The devil is everywhere, the chaos is all around us." That was their big statement, such as it was. Like, "Get over yourselves, folks. There are worse devils than us. We're just a rock 'n' roll band."

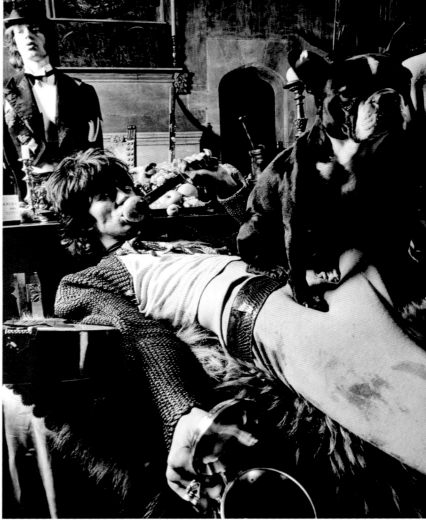

At the photo shoot for the proposed sleeve of *Beggars Banquet*, June 7, 1968.

At the mock banquet to launch *Beggars Banquet*, December 5, 1968.

While the Stones were having food fights, the cracks in the Beatles armor were widening. Tom Hanley made these images inside the Apple offices on Saville Row in 1969.

The honeymooning Ono and Lennon protest inside the Amsterdam Hilton, March 1969. Lennon was putting himself on the line—something the Stones simply didn't do.

JD: Lennon was doing more than just playing in a rock 'n' roll band. When you look at it now, it might seem pretty silly to stage a "bed-in," as he did in Montreal and Amsterdam with Yoko in 1969, and think that it will stop the war in Vietnam, but Lennon was very much confronting political issues. As we said when we talked about "Revolution" (see Chapter Five), he didn't see any easy answers, and he wasn't endorsing anyone's ten-point plan, but he *was* putting himself on the line— perhaps much to the embarrassment of McCartney. The Stones simply didn't do that, ever, not even after Altamont. And we really have to talk about how that mess changed the perception of them.

GK: The year leading up to that free concert in California in December 1969 saw the Stones oust Brian Jones and bring in Mick Taylor as guitarist. He made his first contribution on "Honky Tonk Women" in the spring of 1969, continuing the band's rock 'n' roll renaissance. Taylor made his live debut with the band in Hyde Park in July 1969, only days after Jones was found dead in his pool. The technical prowess and professional reliability of Taylor enabled them to get back on the road. Poor Brian Jones was already an afterthought when he died.

JD: I just have to insert here that Robert Johnson, I suspect, knew quite well what he did when he sold his soul to the devil at the crossroads. Poor Mick Taylor—I don't think he ever knew what he was getting into!

GK: Yeah, I'm not sure he was even that enamored with the band, but it was a good gig . . . or it seemed like a good gig at the time.

JD: But he would barely survive!

Hyde Park, July 5, 1969, just days after Jones was found dead in his pool at Cotchford Farm. The show was Taylor's live Stones debut.

Hyde Park. These weren't your California Hells Angels, as the Stones would find out five months later.

GK: Yeah, I'm not sure he ever got the license plate on that bus that ran him over, but for a while there, he added a lot to this band musically. It really opened up the possibilities in their sound in ways that Jones was no longer physically or psychologically able to.

JD: Plus the Stones' dynamic had shifted: Jones always considered the Stones to be his band, and Stanley Booth really does a good job of portraying that in *The True Adventures of the Rolling Stones*. But it was never going to be his band again once you had the ascendance of the Glimmer Twins songwriting team, Jagger and Richards. Taylor, as talented as he was, simply was a tool for Richards and Jagger to use.

GK: But what a tool! You look at the Stones' productivity during this time, and it was awe-inspiring. It may be the best four-album run in rock history, starting with *Beggars Banquet* in 1968 and ending with *Exile on Main St.* in 1972. *Let It Bleed* arrived in 1969, conveniently timed to the end of the Sixties, and just as the Stones were about to enter that cesspool of violence and murder that was Altamont. Intentionally or not, *Let It Bleed* is a brilliant reflection on the collapse of that era. Can you think of a better epitaph for the Sixties than "You Can't Always Get What You Want"?

Capitalizing on negative energy: the Stones at Altamont Speedway, December 6, 1969.

JD: Two things about Altamont that I think are always overlooked in the mythologizing of that event: One, no less a critic than Lester Bangs, who loved the Stones and had seen them several times by that point, said that they had never sounded better than they did on stage that day. A lot of bands take the positive energy of the audience and amplify it and become all the better for it in a classic feedback loop. The Stones could take *negative* energy and use it even more effectively than good vibes! Two, for all of the terror that is present at Altamont and so visible in *Gimme Shelter*, the incredible documentary where you see the Hells Angels beating Meredith Hunter to death, you have to remember that only one of the assailants was ever identified and

indicted, that his lawyer argued self-defense, and that a jury of his peers acquitted him—in one of the most conservative courts in California!

GK: It was a travesty all around. The movie was an indictment not only of that event—the incredible amount of stupidity and lack of forethought that went into it—but also of the Stones and their jaded, almost disinterested reaction to how it all went down. They were understandably a little gun-shy, given their prior experiences with the legal system in England, but here they did everything they could to distance themselves from the tragedy, as if what happened had nothing to do with them.

A film still and ad proofs from *Gimme Shelter,* the Maysles brothers' documentary that was an indictment not just of the Hells Angels, but also the Stones and their jaded, almost disinterested reaction to how Altamont all went down.

That stance, of course, only enhanced their image as evil incarnate. It made them even more alluring and notorious. They were the gangsta rappers of their day, a force far more divisive than the Beatles. Lennon on his own was a magnet for controversy, but the Beatles collectively were no match for the Stones as rock 'n' roll outlaws.

JD: And rightfully so. Writing about the tour that followed that 1969 jaunt, Lester Bangs was really distressed to see that the Stones were now celebutantes, separated from their audience, no longer of the people, and essentially happy to have become everything they once mocked and hated. It was the start of the situation that exists today, where they are this mega-corporation that meets every few years to replenish the coffers with a tour based around an absurd new stage, a multimillion-dollar production, and a new album that's essentially just a concert souvenir, and it all has very little or nothing to do with the desire to perform and connect with the audience. The early Seventies were the beginning of the end for them as a live act, but they still managed to produce several of their best albums before they ran out of steam as a truly inspired and creative unit in the studio.

The hiring of New York–based manager Allen Klein widened the rift between McCartney and the rest of the Beatles.

The album that morphed from the premise of no overdubs to a Phil Spector super-production more than a year after it was recorded.

Eastman and Eastman
39 West 54th Street
New York
New York 10019

18th April 1969

Attention Lee Eastman, Esq.

Dear Mr. Eastman,

    This is to inform you of the fact that you are not authorized to act or to hold yourself out as the attourney or legal representative of "The Beatles" or of any of the companies which the Beatles own or control.

    We recognize that you are authorized to act for Paul McCartney, personally, and in this regard we will instruct our representatives to give you the fullest co-operation.

    We would appreciate your forwarding to

    ABKCO Industries Inc.
    1700 Broadway
    New York
    N.Y.

all documents, correspondence and files which you hold in your possession relating to the affairs of the Beatles, or any of the companies which the Beatles own or control.

    Very truly yours,

John Lennon

Richard Starkey

George Harrison

McCartney reacted to the hiring of Klein by hiring his father-in-law, Lee Eastman, as his business manager. This letter from the rest of the band is evidence that their managerial situation was a major catalyst in their breakup.

160

After the *Let It Be* sessions of 1968 and early 1969, the Beatles brought Martin back into the fold in the spring and summer of 1969 for the *Abbey Road* sessions.

GK: The Beatles hit the studio wall in January 1969 during the *Let It Be* sessions. McCartney's idea was, "Let's try to do a show, boys!" He was trying to get them back to the spirit of '64, when they were a working road band. That didn't work, so instead of the lead-in to a concert, the rehearsals became a live-in-the-studio record. Lennon was certainly in favor of that. He detested some of the more elaborate studio experiments that had come to dominate the last few Beatles albums. Yoko is sitting in John's lap during the sessions, and the other three are wondering what the hell is going on. Harrison continues to feel like a stepchild in this band, with his songs nitpicked by the others and his playing belittled. It was a misguided project from the start. It started with this premise of "no overdubs," and it ended up being a Phil Spector super-production by the time they were done with it more than a year later.

JD: The Stones dropped *Beggars Banquet* in December 1968, and, hands down, it's a more impressive record than the White Album. The next year, 1969, found the Beatles trying mightily to recover their mojo with *Let It Be*, but it wasn't quite working, as you said—and I have to add that the *Let It Be . . . Naked* re-release in 2003 shed no light on what they were really trying to do back then. In fact, I think it kills the argument that it was

Spector, who had been recruited by Lennon, who ruined that record. It just really wasn't that great to begin with! A lot of what Spector did gets a bad rap. I don't mind his version of "Across the Universe" at all, for example.

GK: *Let It Be . . . Naked* was McCartney's way of getting the last word. Lennon heaped praise on Spector for "saving" the album; McCartney hated Spector's orchestrations and preferred the original sound, hence the release of *Naked*. Besides the aesthetic conflicts, there was also the disarray in the Beatles' Apple Records company. They hire Allen Klein, again a sore point between Lennon and McCartney, and he begins dismantling Apple. He fires some of the band's most trusted aides, like Alistair Taylor, who had accompanied Brian Epstein to the Cavern Club in 1962 when Epstein decided to manage the band. The business foundation is being pulled out from under them. McCartney sees the band slipping away and takes one last stab at pulling it all together. He wants to go back to the days of *Sgt. Pepper's* and *Revolver*, and "make a record like we used to." They call up Martin, bring him back into the fold, and end up working on the *Abbey Road* album in the spring and summer of 1969, which would prove to be their last hurrah together in the studio.

Lennon in 1969, reinvigorated after a year in which heroin and general dissatisfaction with the status quo had taken their toll.

162

Abbey Road and the Iain Macmillan photograph that has inspired thousands of imitators.

A major factor in *Abbey Road*. After years of fighting to get his songs on albums, Harrison's attitude toward Lennon and McCartney had hardened.

JD: *Let It Be* wouldn't come out until May 1970, but *Abbey Road* was the last album they recorded. How do we explain this final triumph when there hadn't been much at all working for the Beatles in those last few years?

GK: As Lennon's mood goes, so go the Beatles. He was actually pretty eager to get back into the studio and do some good work. He had songs piling up, and he was reinvigorated after a year where Yoko, heroin, and his general dissatisfaction with the status quo really took a toll on his Beatles' ambitions. "Come Together" illustrates that, for a brief moment, anyway, these guys were still capable of working together at a very high level. Lennon had been messing around with a campaign slogan that acid guru Timothy Leary was going to use for the 1968 presidential campaign. He tosses in a little Chuck Berry reference in the lyric, *"Here come old flat-top."* The swampy groove is carried by McCartney's bass line.

It was a genuine latter-day collaboration between two guys who really weren't the best of friends anymore. It's a final "Let's win one for the Gipper" moment for them.

The other major factor in this album is Harrison's songwriting. All that mental abuse from his band mates had really hardened his attitude toward them, and it freed him up, in a way. He ended up writing two of the best songs of his or the Beatles' catalog with "Something" and "Here Comes the Sun."

"Something" is the equal of any ballad that McCartney did. There is an intrinsic beauty to that song that never fades. "Here Comes the Sun" is Harrison singing to himself, in a way. He's strolling in Eric Clapton's garden, the clouds are parting, and the sun is finding its way through at last—that's George's way of dealing with all the put-downs and hurt he feels and telling himself it's going to be all right. The guitar lick that he plays behind the mantra of *"Sun, sun, sun"* is classic Harrison, a signature moment every bit as great as his opening chord in "A Hard Day's Night."

Stones in the studio, 1969.

McCartney and Linda Eastman enter the Marylebone Register Office by the side door for their civil marriage ceremony, March 12, 1969.

Lennon and Ono wave their marriage certificate after their wedding on Gibraltar, March 20, 1969.

Starr on the set of the film *The Magic Christian*, September 1969.

Harrison performs with Delaney & Bonnie, Copenhagen, Denmark, December 1969.

AND IN THE END, THE LOVE YOU MAKE . . . ETC., ETC. ∘ 165

Starr, Harrison, and Lennon watch Bob Dylan and The Band perform at the Isle of Wight Festival, August 31, 1969.

JD: With "Maxwell's Silver Hammer," McCartney doesn't fare as well as Harrison. It's another of his music-hall toss-offs, along with being a really weird song essentially glorifying a serial killer. Paul, what's that about? And "Oh! Darling" just sucks. But the whole second half of the album after "Here Comes the Sun" is what *Sgt. Pepper's* was intended to be, only much better. You have a lot of flotsam and jetsam from Lennon's notebook and McCartney's stash of tunes—half-finished songs, ideas that are strong for a minute and half but don't really flesh out for a three-minute song—so what do they do? They tie them all together. Brilliant!

GK: Yeah, and they create one of the first side-long rock suites. Plus, there was some bite there too. In songs like "You Never Give Me Your Money" or "Carry That Weight," McCartney was doing a little venting at the expense of Allen Klein. A state of discord and disarray inspired brilliant music—again an example of the band

members rallying themselves to make an album worthy of their legacy, in spite of the turmoil around them.

JD: Then there's Lennon doing his social critique thing with "Mean Mr. Mustard" and "Polythene Pam," sneering at straight society. He'd do a lot more of that without the cute metaphors on his solo albums, but it's nice to hear that snarling energy and anger. What I could do without is "The End" and "Her Majesty," both classic cases of McCartney schlock.

GK: Wrong, wrong, wrong! "The End" ties the album together. Is there any greater closing couplet than *"And, in the end, the love you take/Is equal to the love you make"*? That's one way to look at the Beatles' entire career.

JD: Well, even if I were to buy that, Paul ruins it with the twenty-three-second coda of "Her Majesty."

Just two weeks before the release of *Abbey Road* in September 1969, Lennon's first live performance in three years was not with the Beatles, but with the Plastic Ono Band. They're seen here after their September 13, 1969, performance at the Toronto Rock and Roll Revival. From left: Alan White, Eric Clapton (seated), Klaus Voorman, Lennon, and Ono.

The Plastic Ono Band plays the U.N. Children's Fund Concert at the Lyceum, London, December 16, 1969.

GK: C'mon, you're talking about twenty-three seconds! Gimme a break! And what about McCartney's bass-playing on this album? You could do a clinic on that. Ringo's drumming is just as remarkable. His drum solo on "The End" is yet another reason that song ranks with the greatest Beatles moments.

JD: He plays his first and only Beatles' drum solo—actually, more of a focused and melodic fill—and it's absolutely perfect. Plus, there is the sound of the *Abbey Road* record. I think, post-psychedelia, that the innovations of *Revolver* and what followed had been so powerful that the Beatles had to have been asking themselves, "What's left for us to do in the studio?" And here they were, especially with something like "She's So Heavy," pretty much setting the templates for the sounds of Seventies rock. There were the roots of heavy

metal, and of the power-pop that would follow later in the decade. *Abbey Road* is a modern-sounding record even now, four decades later.

GK: Yes! So you have this last, grand statement arriving in September 1969, and yet just two weeks before its release, Lennon's first performance in three years is not with the Beatles but with the Plastic Ono Band, consisting of Yoko Ono, Klaus Voorman, Alan White, and Eric Clapton at the Toronto Rock and Roll Revival. Meanwhile, Paul has a four-track recorder installed in his house and starts working on his solo record. The Beatles leave Abbey Road Studio in the summer of 1969 for the last time as a functioning band. Their breakup in 1970 is just a formality, as solo records start filtering out from McCartney, Lennon, Harrison, and even Starr.

A brilliant reflection on the end of the Sixties, conveniently released days before the Stones entered the cesspool of violence that was Altamont. The sculpture was done by renowned Sixties graphic designer Robert Brownjohn.

Richards and Jagger work on *Let It Bleed* with producer Jimmy Miller, Los Angeles, October 1969.

JD: Interestingly enough, the Beatles' breakup was like a nuclear explosion that just obliterated any attention being paid to anything else in the pop world for a time. The Stones didn't release an album in 1970, and it was almost as if they were saying, "Okay, you guys get out of the way before we come back." *Let It Bleed* came out in late 1969, and then 1970 was the story of the Beatles unraveling while the Stones laid low.

GK: In terms of music, yes, but the Stones were otherwise busying themselves with the business of being celebrities who had transcended rock, in a way. They were being written about in the gossip columns and movie sections, and they were being embraced by Hollywood royalty. Jagger had no less than three movies come out in 1970. In the midst of all this, they still found time to record the music for *Sticky Fingers*. It was their first album for Rolling Stones Records, the boutique label Atlantic Records handed them. The band members were in a foul, post-Altamont mood. They were jaded beyond belief, and this album is brimming with the drugs and decadence that were consuming their lives. In a song like "Brown Sugar," they leave no taboo undisturbed: slavery, interracial sex, sadomasochism,

all in one three-minute-fifty-second package! It's the Stones exploiting their post-Altamont reputation as Evildoers, Inc., and rubbing our faces in it.

JD: "We are who we are, and we are a pop product, and we're not going to apologize. In fact, we're going to hire the Pop artist Andy Warhol to design our album cover." It's a brilliant piece of album art with the workable zipper, even if it was the bane of every vinyl LP collector. As soon as they put it in the stack, it ruined the record in front of it! Nevertheless, you pull it down, there is the underwear—what a perfect statement. More importantly, there's no denying that it's a great album. As we've said, it's been hard from the beginning to say how sincere the Stones ever were—how much was Jagger really just trying to push buttons with "Brown Sugar," et cetera. But "Wild Horses" is a beautiful, powerful, moving, and, I think, very heartfelt song. Keith always had fewer problems with sincerity, and "Can't You Hear Me Knocking" and "Bitch" are two of his most direct and best tunes ever.

GK: At the same time, there is a maturity about this record lacking in their earlier work. Listen to the way

Madison Square Garden, New York, November 28, 1969. Ian Stewart, longtime Stones pianist and the man Andrew Loog Oldham sacked from the regular lineup for looking too conservative, is at far left.

Did the Stones position themselves as evil incarnate? Jagger prances across the stage on the Stones' 1969 U.S. tour.

Jagger sings "I Got the Blues," without affectation. In the past, he might have exaggerated his voice on the more traditional-sounding blues and country songs, but this performance is, dare I say it, sincere.

JD: Same for the cover of Mississippi Fred McDowell's "You Gotta Move." And "Dead Flowers" simply is one of the best country-rock songs ever written.

GK: That's just brilliant, though "Dead Flowers" is once again sung in Jagger's exaggerated hillbilly drawl, his equivalent of a teenager rolling his eyes at something he deems woefully unhip. But "Sway" is a great Jagger vocal, where he talks about the cost of living that "demon life." It's not just a sneer; there's a hint of regret there. "Wild Horses" is about missing home, missing your loved ones. Keith Richards is writing about leaving his wife, Anita, and his young son for a Stones tour. "Moonlight Mile" would've been unimaginable a few years earlier—that haunted, world-weary tone. Being on the road, missing home, and not being able to get back there anytime soon—to ward off the pain and loneliness, you numb your body and brain, and you walk through life with a "head full of snow." So amid all of the button-pushing with songs like "Brown Sugar" and "Bitch," where they reduce everyone to a salivating dog in heat, you also get this other level of aching, bone-deep introspection.

JD: Ending with "Moonlight Mile" points to a search for some sort of spiritual transcendence—a way out of the vile, decadent, self-abusive lives they've been living. It's a key song that points to *Exile*, which perfects that theme of being in the darkest place imaginable and seeking the light.

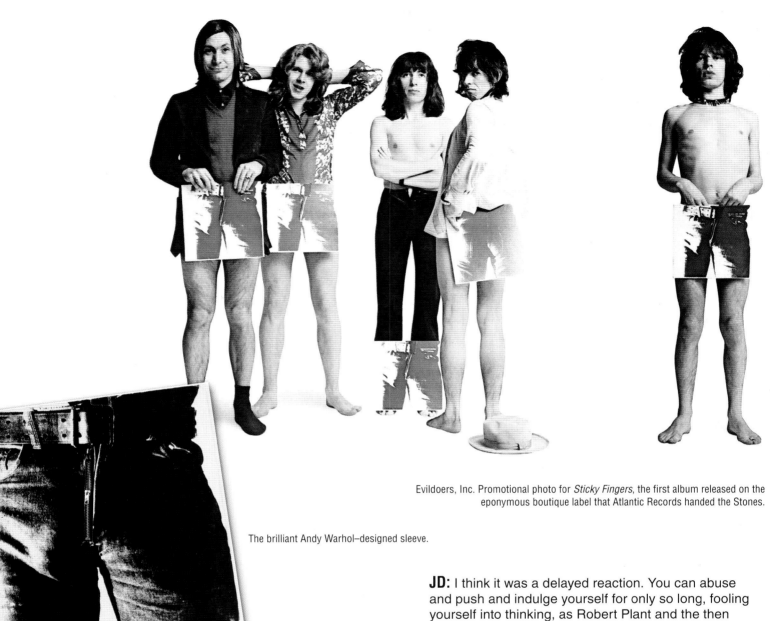

The brilliant Andy Warhol–designed sleeve.

Evildoers, Inc. Promotional photo for *Sticky Fingers*, the first album released on the eponymous boutique label that Atlantic Records handed the Stones.

GK: The Stones were still able to pull out amazing art in the middle of this swirl of star power, celebrity, and cocaine that they were caught up in. One reason was Mick Taylor's brilliance as a guitar player. "Can't You Hear Me Knocking" starts off as this classic Keith riff-rocker and then goes into a Santana-esque, Latin-flavored jam that's a showcase for Taylor as a soloist. That was something the band wasn't capable of a few years earlier. Their ability to stay focused during this time when other bands would've imploded still amazes me.

Do you have a take on why that was? With *Sticky Fingers* and *Exile on Main St.*, there were a lot of reasons why those records should have turned into self-indulgent messes.

JD: I think it was a delayed reaction. You can abuse and push and indulge yourself for only so long, fooling yourself into thinking, as Robert Plant and the then rising Led Zeppelin might have put it, that you're no mere human, you are a Golden God. The Stones were Golden Gods for a while, and then their mortality came crashing home after *Exile* with *Goats Head Soup* in 1973, *It's Only Rock and Roll* in 1974, and *Black and Blue* in 1976. Those albums amplify all of the worst traits bubbling under on *Sticky Fingers*, especially the sexism, but with a lot less inspiration and melody. There are moments, say, with "Angie," but they're fleeting.

GK: I buy that, but I'm still shocked at the suddenness of the decline. You go from *Exile* to *Goats Head Soup* a year later, with a song like "Dancing with Mr. D" that is a parody of the "evil incarnate" trip they were doing much more convincingly with "Sympathy for the Devil." And "Star Star" is just cynical, a lesser version of the "Stray Cat Blues" groupie-sex song. They're repeating themselves, and they sound bored.

While the Stones, as a band, laid low in 1970, Jagger appeared in three films. Here he is on the set of *Performance* with his costar—and Richards' wife—Anita Pallenberg.

McCartney with wife Linda on their rural farm the day before he began court proceedings the seal the Beatles' breakup. Perhaps he's asking that enduring question: "What could have happened if the Beatles had survived?"

JD: When "Sympathy for the Devil" comes together in Jean-Luc Godard's film of the same name, you see the group trying that song with several different grooves before settling into the rhythm that actually makes it. There is still a band that is willing to try a lot of different things in the studio, to test each other and push each other, and then that disappears. You get the impression that Jagger comes in with his songs, Richards comes in with his, and they say, "These are the tunes. Let's just record them so we can go out and make X-million pounds next year on tour." And it's all pro forma instead of a band that is still growing and enjoying working together.

GK: There was no better rock band on the planet between 1968 and 1972, and then the decline was incredibly swift, even though they were still cleaning up on the road.

JD: Absolutely! But here's a fun game: What would have happened if the Beatles had survived?

GK: McCartney clearly was the one most invested in the group in the end, but only if George and Ringo knew their place. And Lennon had clearly tuned everyone out. McCartney did say that it had to be the four of them, or the band was over. There was a brief instant when Harrison left the band, and Lennon blithely said, "Oh, we'll just get Clapton." McCartney, deep in his heart, knew that couldn't be.

JD: Maybe that's the key to why the Stones had a longer run: It just took Jagger and Richards a little longer to hate each other as intensely as McCartney and Lennon! Clearly, starting at some point between *Exile* and *Some Girls* in 1978, there started to be less and less of a

The Stones roll on and pay their respects at the Alamo in San Antonio, Texas, on their Tour of the Americas, June 1975.

connection between Richards and Jagger, with little to none remaining today. Sometimes, they hate each other a little less than other times, and sometimes, it is outright open warfare. Yet they still are always willing to come together for the good of the corporation or their bank accounts.

GK: If you look at the Stones after the mid-Eighties, they have been making one White Album after another. The two principal songwriters in the band rarely come into the studio together anymore to create music. They are basically using the Stones as a glorified backing band, so it's not really a band in the traditional sense anymore.

JD: But what if Lennon and McCartney had been able to have the corporate mindset and continue to put out product? The other guys probably would not have indulged George in doing something as sprawling as *All Things Must Pass*. Lennon might not have been allowed to revel in his nostalgic fondness for the sounds that first inspired him, as he did with *Rock 'n' Roll*. There would still have been some sort of check on McCartney's cheesiness. . . .

GK: I could certainly see some of McCartney's solo and Wings stuff winding up on Beatles albums, but

Lennon would've destroyed him for doing something like "My Love." McCartney probably wouldn't have tolerated the Lennon of the *Plastic Ono Band* album, either—they were too personal, and too emotionally intense. The others would've viewed that music as an indulgence. And I doubt Ringo's cover of the "No No Song" would've made the cut either. See what we would've missed?

Let's go make X-million pounds. Portfolio belonging to the Stones' accountant on the 1975 Tour of the Americas.

NO MOSS

THE BEST OF *SOME GIRLS* AND BEYOND

by Greg Kot

In 1978, the Rolling Stones got it together for one last blast of brilliance. *Some Girls* proved to be a summing up of everything that was great about the band, a compendium of their best moves. It didn't break ground, but it didn't have to. Forged in the immediate aftermath of punk and the rise of such bands as the Sex Pistols and the Clash, it was spiked with dirty guitars and dirtier songs. The album feels rude, almost dashed off. "When the Whip Comes Down" is as savage as any Stones song has ever sounded. The black comedy of the title track presages Eminem and N.W.A. A guitar solo barges through a cover of the Temptations' "Just My Imagination (Running Away with Me)" like a foul-mouthed drunk.

The Stones were once again relevant with "Miss You," a single that ruled the summer of 1978. The quintet was justifiably proud of the album. When they played Soldier Field in Chicago soon after the album was released, they played nine of the album's ten songs—try imagining any stadium rock band doing that today.

The album was steered by Mick Jagger, with Keith Richards distracted by drug addiction and legal problems. Richards wrote "Beast of Burden" in response—as close to an apology as he ever gave his fellow Glimmer Twin. And on an album laden with bile, misogyny, cynicism (the usual Stones fare, in other words), Richards uncorks the most heartfelt moment on his outlaw anthem "Before They Make Me Run": *"Watched my taillights fading/Not a dry eye in the house that I can see."*

But the Stones didn't fade away. The music, however, has been in steady decline. After *Some Girls*, the Stones had no more album-length masterpieces left in them. But they did have their moments over the last three decades on a series of mostly indifferent studio albums. Here are the keepers.

"EMOTIONAL RESCUE" *(1980)*
This neo-disco workout has Jagger at his leering, falsetto-voiced, tongue-in-cheek best, spinning a ridiculously hilarious tale over a great Ronnie Wood bass line.

"SHE'S SO COLD" *(1980)*
As direct as a slap in the face.

One last blast of brilliance, forged in the immediate aftermath of punk. A steady decline followed.

"START ME UP" *(1981)*
The last of the all-time great Keith Richards riffs.

"WAITING ON A FRIEND" *(1981)*
A rare moment of tenderness, punctuated by a Sonny Rollins saxophone solo.

"HAD IT WITH YOU" *(1986)*
In one of their most fallow periods, the Stones reach back for some Chuck Berry–like rock 'n' roll and vent their animosity toward one another.

"THRU AND THRU" *(1994)*
Increasingly, Richards' ravaged vocal turns have become the heart and soul of the Stones in their latter years.

"YOU DON'T HAVE TO MEAN IT" *(1997)*
Roots, rock, and now reggae, courtesy of Keith.

"BACK OF MY HAND" *(2005)*
Back to the Chicago blues, and it grinds with hypnotic authority.

The Stones' famous benefit show for the Canadian National Institute for the Blind, Oshawa, Ontario, April 22, 1979.

SO ALONE

THE BEST OF THE SOLO BEATLES

by Greg Kot

JOHN LENNON

"COLD TURKEY" *(1969)*
Scorched-earth method acting as Lennon relives the anguish of withdrawal.

"INSTANT KARMA" *(1970)*
Slamming, Phil Spector–produced wall of sound that shouts, "We all shine on!"

Plastic Ono Band *(1970)*
An exorcism. "The dream is over," Lennon sang, and it was.

Imagine *(1971)*
Though the title song is hippie hokum, Lennon delivers the goods in the self-lacerating "Jealous Guy" and the snarling "Gimme Some Truth."

"#9 DREAM" *(1975)*
A strangely moving and ambitious visitation from the muse that inspired "I Am the Walrus" and "Strawberry Fields Forever."

"STAND BY ME" *(1975)*
To woo back Yoko Ono, Lennon conjures the soul singer within on this pleading cover of Ben E. King's classic ballad.

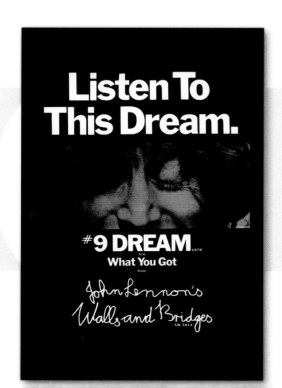

"HELP ME TO HELP MYSELF" *(2000)*
A previously unreleased demo that surfaced on the reissue of his final album, the 1980 release *Double Fantasy*. Lennon alone at the piano offers a haunting premonition: *"Well I tried so hard to settle down/But the angel of destruction keeps on/Houndin' me all around."*

PAUL McCARTNEY

"MAYBE I'M AMAZED" *(1970)*
In soul-ballad mode, McCartney delivers the sole keeper from his undercooked solo debut album.

"UNCLE ALBERT/ADMIRAL HALSEY" *(1971)*
The very sort of thing that made Lennon run for the hills in the Beatles' latter days. In retrospect, it's an elaborate, inscrutable goof with a dazzling arrangement.

WINGS, *Band on the Run* *(1973)*
With Wings, McCartney makes this a near-masterpiece, his pop instincts in the multipart title track and soul-fired "Let Me Roll It" balanced by rock grit.

"SILLY LOVE SONGS" *(1976)*
Routinely cited as Exhibit A when Paul detractors discuss his Wings-era output, McCartney's brilliant disco-era bass line is anything but trivial.

WINGS, *Wings over America* *(1977)*
In the era of bloated multidisc live albums, this toughens up McCartney's sound, making this far preferable to most of his overly polite studio albums.

Chaos and Creation in the Back Yard *(2005)*
Designed to evoke the intimate, one-man-band feel of his 1970 solo debut and its 1980 successor, *McCartney II*, this album is much better than either. Thirteen ballads and smaller mood pieces add up to Paul's best work in decades.

Memory Almost Full *(2007)*
McCartney creates a sweeping soundtrack for heavier-than-usual subject matter as he looks back on his childhood, ruminates about love lost, and even envisions his funeral.

THE FIREMAN, *Electric Arguments* *(2008)*
With the producer Youth, McCartney indulges his more experimental impulses as "The Fireman." The duo's third release is an accomplished combination of melody and experimental mirth.

Fresh McCartney!

GEORGE HARRISON

All Things Must Pass (1970)
The guitarist's first post-Beatles album is stuffed with songs his former band mates rejected. Their loss. As solo Beatles recordings go, this is in the top two, jousting it out with Lennon's *Plastic Ono Band*. It's all orchestrated into cathedral-rock splendor by Phil Spector.

"CRACKERBOX PALACE" (1976)
The self-serious one delivers a song that twinkles with good humor.

"THIS SONG" (1976)
Best song ever about a copyright lawsuit, commenting on the "My Sweet Lord" court battle successfully waged against Harrison by the songwriters of the Chiffons' "He's So Fine."

"HERE COMES THE MOON" (1979)
The enchanting response to "Here Comes the Sun," in the wake of the guitarist's marriage to Olivia Arias and the birth of their son, Dhani.

"ALL THOSE YEARS AGO" (1981)
A rare reunion with McCartney and Starr results in a moving reflection on Beatlemania in the immediate aftermath of John Lennon's murder.

Cloud Nine (1987)
A midcareer renaissance with Eric Clapton on guitar, Ringo

Saturday Night Live, November 19, 1976.

on drums, and Elton John helping out on keyboards. Harrison touches all the key bases: pop exuberance (his cover of James Ray's 1962 hit "Got My Mind Set on You"), affectionate nostalgia ("When We Was Fab"), rock be-bop-a-lula ("Devil's Radio"), and stately reflection ("Just for Today").

THE TRAVELING WILBURYS, *Vol. 1* (1988)
Harrison joins Bob Dylan, Roy Orbison, Tom Petty, and Jeff Lynne for a loose, breezy set that holds up much better than most supergroup collaborations.

RINGO STARR

"IT DON'T COME EASY" (1971)
Though Ringo scored seven top-ten singles in the Seventies, this is the only one you need, a solid rocker with plenty of help from George Harrison, who played guitar in addition to co-writing and producing it.

Recording sessions for B. B. King in London, Command Studios, 1971.

HE'S DECIDED . . .

SHE'S *DEFINITELY* DECIDED . . .

SO WHAT WOULD *YOU* RATHER BE . . .

A BEATLE . . . .

. . . OR A STONE?

ACKNOWLEDGMENTS

MUCH GRATITUDE to our editor, Dennis Pernu, and publisher, Michael Dregni, at Voyageur Press for their guidance and enthusiasm. We owe Jenny Grandy big-time for her research, transcriptions, editing assistance, and scrupulous attention to detail. Props to my editors at the *Chicago Tribune*, especially Scott Powers, for helping me shape a career out of my two great passions: music and writing. To our gifted *Sound Opinions* co-producers, Jason Saldanha and Robin Linn, thanks for always having our backs. To my brilliant parents, Len and June, thanks for letting me turn the family stereo up—loud! (And, Mom, I forgive you for making me take down that Stones poster on my bedroom wall.) As usual, my wife, Deb, and daughters, Katie and Marissa, not only put up with my prolonged absences in the midst of another book project but cheered me on. Wild horses couldn't drag me away from you.

—*Greg Kot*

IN ADDITION TO seconding my colleague's heartfelt thanks to everyone at Voyageur Press and *Sound Opinions*, I have to underscore that we could not have done this book without the help of Jenny Grandy, who's soon to become a no-doubt killer attorney. I also have to thank my lovely wife, Carmél Carrillo (a major, major George fan); our daughter, Melody Rose (who loves the Beatles, though the Stones still scare her, thank goodness); my parents, Helene and Harry Reynolds (who not only endured the blasting stereo for all of those years but put up with the rattling drum set in the basement trying to master "Ticket to Ride" and the intro of "Honky Tonk Women"); and my old college buddy, Tony "A. J." DiMurro, now a talented playwright but then the Virgil guiding me through what would become a lifelong fascination with the Stones at their most decadent and hardest-rocking.

—*Jim DeRogatis*

SELECT BIBLIOGRAPHY

Booth, Stanley. *The True Adventures of the Rolling Stones*. London: Heinemann, 1985.

Brown, Peter and Steven Gaines. *The Love You Make: An Insider's Story of the Beatles*. New York: McGraw-Hill, 1983.

Davis, Stephen. *Old Gods Almost Dead: The 40-Year Odyssey of the Rolling Stones*. New York: Broadway, 2001.

Editors of *Rolling Stone*. *Harrison*. New York: Simon & Schuster, 2002.

Elliott, Martin. *The Rolling Stones Complete Recording Sessions*. London: Blandford, 1990.

Emerick, Geoff and Massey, Howard. *Here, There, and Everywhere: My Life Recording the Music of the Beatles*. New York: Gotham, 2006.

Goldman, Albert. *The Lives of John Lennon*. New York: Morrow, 1988.

Greenfield, Robert. *S.T.P.: A Journey through America with the Rolling Stones*. New York: Saturday Review Press, 1974.

Hertsgaard, Mark. *A Day in the Life: The Music and Artistry of the Beatles*. New York: Delacorte Press, 1995.

Lewisohn, Mark. *The Complete Beatles Recording Sessions: The Official Abbey Road Studio Session Notes, 1962–1970*. London: Hamlyn, 1988.

MacDonald, Ian. *Revolution in the Head: The Beatles' Records and the Sixties*. New York: Henry Holt, 1994.

O'Donnell, Jim. *The Day John Met Paul: An Hour-by-Hour Account of How the Beatles Began*. New York: Penguin, 1996.

Pallington West, Jessica. *What Would Keith Richards Do? Daily Affirmations from a Rock 'n' Roll Survivor*. New York: Bloomsbury USA, 2009.

Phelge, James. *Nankering with the Rolling Stones: The Untold Story of the Early Days*. Chicago: A Cappella Books, 1998.

Riley, Tim: *Tell Me Why: The Beatles: Album by Album, Song by Song, the Sixties and After*. New York: Knopf, 1988.

Spitz, Bob. *The Beatles: The Biography*. New York: Little, Brown and Co., 2005.

Wenner, Jann. *Lennon Remembers: The Full* Rolling Stone *Interviews from 1970*. New York: Fawcett, 1972.

Wyman, Bill with Ray Coleman. *Stone Alone: The Story of a Rock 'n' Roll Band*. New York: Viking, 1990.

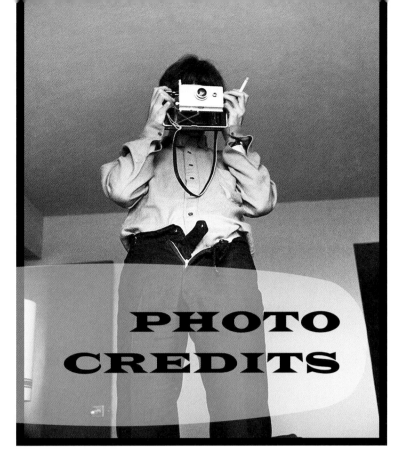

PHOTO CREDITS

CAMERA PRESS LONDON: p82, Peter Shillingford; p89, Wallace Heaton; p160; John Kelly/JBA (top). **CORBIS:** p50, Pierre Fournier/Sygma; p114, Robert Landau (main); p115, Bettmann; p120, Bettmann; p178, Neal Preston. **GETTY IMAGES:** Front Cover, David Farrell/Redferns (Beatles), GAB Archive/Redferns (Rolling Stones); p2, Keystone Features/Hulton Archive; p5, Central Press (main), Hulton Archive (caricature pins); p6, Michael Ochs Archives; p8, Popperfoto (top), Michael Ochs Archives (bottom); p17, John Dominis/Time & Life Pictures (top), Michael Ochs Archives (bottom); p18, Vecchio/Three Lions/Hulton Archive (left), Astrid Kirchherr–K&K/Redferns (right); p19, Michael Ochs Archives (right); p20, George Freston/Fox Photos (left), Harry Benson/Hulton Archive (right lower); p21, Chris Ware/Hulton Archive (left); p22, Bob Grant/Fotos International; p23, John Hoppy Hopkins/Redferns (left), Chris Ware/Hulton Archive (right); p24, GAB Archive/Redferns (top left); p25, GAB Archive/Redferns (bottom left, top right); p28, Keystone Features/Hulton Archive (right); p29, Michael Ochs Archives (upper left, all lower), Three Lions/Hulton Archive (upper middle), Art Shay/Time & Life Pictures (upper right); p30, Michael Ochs Archives (main); p32, *Evening Standard* (main), Hulton Archive (top right, bottom right), GAB Archive/Redferns (bottom left); p33, Keystone Features/Hulton Archive (main), Sammlung Blaschke–K&K/Redferns (top right), Hulton Archive (bottom left, bottom right); p34, William Lovelace/Express; p37, Ulf Kruger OHG–K&K/Redferns (both); p39, Keystone Features/Hulton Archive (main), Michael Ochs Archives (upper); p40–41, Michael Ochs Archives; p42, GAB Archive/Redferns (top); p45, Larry Ellis/Hulton Archive (top), Andrew Maclear/Hulton Archive (bottom); p46, Tom Hanley/Redferns; p47, David Redfern/Redferns; p48, Jan Persson/Redferns; p49 (Ralph Morse/Time & Life Pictures); p51, Terry O'Neill; p52, Walter Iooss Jr. (left); p53, Robert Knight Archive/Redferns; p54, Hulton Archive; p55, Robert Whitaker/Hulton Archive; p55–57, Les Lee/Hulton Archive; p58, Bob Gomel/Time & Life Pictures; p59, Hulton Archive (main); p62, GAB Archive/Redferns; p63, Jan Olofsson/Redferns; p64, Michael Ochs Archives; p65, David Redfern/Redferns; p66, David Redfern/Redferns (main); p67, Ron Howard/Redferns (main), GAB Archive/Redferns (left); p68–69, Robert Whitaker/Hulton Archive; p70, Robert Whitaker/Hulton Archive (main), Michael Ochs Archives (upper); p72, GAB Archive/Redferns (top left, bottom left); p74, George Stroud/Express (main), Michael Ochs Archives (upper left); p75, Larry Ellis/Express (main); p76, BIPS/Hulton Archive (main); p77, John Reader/Time & Life Pictures (left), GAB Archive/Redferns (right); p78, GAB Archive/Redferns; p79, Mark and Colleen Hayward (top), Robert Whitaker/Hulton Archive (lower); p80, Hulton Archive; p83, Jan Persson/Redferns (top left), Walter Daran/Time & Life Pictures (top right), Ivan Keeman/Redferns (bottom left); p84, Robert Whitaker/Hulton Archive (upper), Michael Ochs Archives (lower); p85, Ebet Roberts/Redferns (top left, bottom right), Michael Ochs Archives (top right), Michael Putland/Hulton Archive (bottom left); p86, Redferns; p87, Waring Abbott (main); p88, Chris Ware/Hulton Archive; p90, *Evening Standard* (top), Keystone Features/Hulton Archive (bottom); p91, Keystone Features/Hulton Archive (top), Peter Francis/Redferns (bottom); p92, David Redfern/Redferns; p93, Marty Temme/WireImage (top), Christopher Simon Sykes/Hulton Archive (lower); p94, David Redfern/Redferns (top left), Michael Ochs Archives (top right, bottom left), Bernie Walters–Treecastle Images/Redferns (bottom right); p95, Popperfoto (top left, bottom left), Ulf Kruger OHG–K&K/Redferns (top right), Robert Whitaker/Hulton Archive (bottom right); p96, Richard E. Aaron/Redferns; p97, Christopher Simon Sykes/Hulton Archive; p98, David Redfern/Redferns; p99, Ulf Kruger OHG–K&K/Redferns (main); p100, Christopher Simon Sykes/Hulton Archive; p101, David Redfern/Redferns (top), Graham Wiltshire/Redferns (bottom); p102, Michael Ochs Archives; p103, Bert Kaempfert Music–K&K/Redferns (top left), Robert Whitaker/Hulton Archive (top right), Michael Ochs Archives (bottom); p106, Popperfoto; p107–108, Elliott Landy/Redferns; p112, Michael Ochs Archives (top left, top right), GAB Archive (lower left), Estate of Keith Morris/Redferns (lower right); p113, Estate of Keith Morris/Redferns; p116, Robert Altman/Michael Ochs Archives (top), Keystone Features/Hulton Archive (bottom); p117, Cummings Archives/Redferns (both); p118, Ted West/Hulton Archive (both); p119, Cummings Archives/Redferns (top), *Evening Standard* (bottom); p121, *Evening Standard* (upper left), Jim Gray/Hulton Archive (lower left), Astrid Kirchherr–K&K/Redferns (right); p123, David Redfern/Redferns; p124, Michael Ochs Archives; p125, Christopher Simon Sykes/Hulton Archive; p126, Astrid Kirchherr–K&K/Redferns (top left), Popperfoto (top right), Robert Whitaker/Hulton Archive (bottom left), David Redfern/Redferns (bottom right); p127, Chris Ware/Hulton Archive (top left), Ulf Kruger OHG–K&K/Redferns (top right), Jan Persson/Redferns (bottom left), Richard Upper (bottom right); p128, Michael Ochs Archives; p129, David Redfern/Redferns; p131, Hulton Archive; p132, Fiona Adams/Redferns; p133, Hulton Archive; p134, Michael Ochs Archives (top left, bottom), GAB Archive (top right); p135, Michael Ochs Archive (top), Popperfoto (bottom); p136, Michael Ochs Archives (both); p137, Peter Francis/Redferns; p138, John Reader/Time & Life Pictures; p139, Michael Ochs Archives; p140, Peter Francis/Redferns; p141, David Farrell/Redferns; p142, Val Wilmer/Redferns (top left), Ivan Keeman/Redferns (right); p143, Hulton Archive (main); p144, Robert Whitaker/Hulton Archive; p145, Walter Daran/Time & Life Pictures; p146, Hulton Archive; p147, Popperfoto; p148, Robert Altman/Michael Ochs Archives; p150, Hulton Archive (pins), Redferns (bottom left); p151, Hulton Archive; p153, Popperfoto (right); p154, Mark and Colleen Hayward (top, bottom right), Keystone Features/Hulton Archive (bottom left); p155, Tom Hanley/Redferns (all); p156, Popperfoto; p158, Robert Altman/Michael Ochs Archives; p159, 20th Century Fox/Hulton Archive (top); p160 (lower left); p162, Tom Hanley/Redferns; p163, Tom Hanley/Redferns (right); p164, Michael Ochs Archives (all); p165, Bentley Archive/Popperfoto (top left), Hulton Archive (top right), Ron Galella/WireImage (bottom left), Keystone/Hulton Archive (bottom right); p166, Jeffrey Mayer/WireImage (both); p167, Mark and Colleen Hayward (top), Andrew Maclear/Redferns (lower); p168, Robert Altman/Michael Ochs Archives (main), Redferns (lower); p170, Andrew Maclear/Hulton Archive; p171, Michael Ochs Archives (main); p172, Michael Ochs Archives; p175, Richard E. Aaron/Redferns; p177, Richard E. Aaron/Redferns (top right), Estate of Keith Morris/Redferns (bottom right); p179, Max Scheler–K&K/Redferns; p181, Astrid Kirchherr–K&K/Redferns; p182, John Hoppy Hopkins/Redferns; p184, Michael Ochs Archives; p185–186, Robert Whitaker; p192, Fox Photos/Hulton Archive (top), Ted West/Hulton Archive (bottom). **THE HAYWARD ARCHIVE (ROCKMUSICPRINTS.COM):** p27 (top); p81, Estate of Cecil Beaton; p152. **MIRRORPIX:** p21 (right); p26 (upper); p31 (left); p35 (lower); p36 (main); p71; p83 (center, bottom right); p109–111; p122; p149–150 (top); p157 (all); p161; p173 (top). **KEITH SALENGER COLLECTION:** p87 (inset); p173 (bottom).

Born in Jersey City, New Jersey, the year the Beatles arrived in America, **Jim DeRogatis** began voicing his opinions about rock 'n' roll shortly thereafter. A full-time member of the English Department faculty at Columbia College Chicago, he also blogs about popular music for Vocalo.org. He spent fifteen years as the pop music critic at the *Chicago Sun-Times*, and has written several books about music, including *Let It Blurt: The Life and Times of Lester Bangs, America's Greatest Rock Critic*; *Staring at Sound: The True Story of Oklahoma's Fabulous Flaming Lips*; and *Turn On Your Mind: Four Decades of Great Psychedelic Rock*. DeRogatis lives on the North Side of Chicago with his wife, Carmél, near their daughter, Melody, and he jokes that he is not a musician, but he *is* a drummer. Visit him on the web at www.jimdero.com.

The music critic at the *Chicago Tribune* since 1990, **Greg Kot** has written several books, including *Wilco: Learning How to Die* and *Ripped: How the Wired Generation Revolutionized Music*. He has contributed to numerous other magazines and books, including *Harrison: A* Rolling Stone *Tribute to George Harrison*. In his spare time, Kot is a youth basketball coach and is the coauthor of *Survival Guide for Coaching Youth Basketball*. He has lived on Chicago's Northwest Side through numerous character-building winters with his wife, Deb, two daughters, and far too many records. You can contact him via www.gregkot.com.

About SOUND OPINIONS

Together, Kot and DeRogatis have hosted *Sound Opinions*, "the world's only rock 'n' roll talk show," since 1999. The weekly hour-long music-geek fest originates at Chicago Public Radio and is distributed nationally—from the Bronx to Unalaska, and from Northern Minnesota to Dallas, Texas. You can read more about the program, stream the audio, or download the podcast on the web at www.soundopinions.org.

SONG & LP INDEX

INDEX